The
FOUNDATION OF
MANAGEMENT

The
FOUNDATION OF
MANAGEMENT

P. D. ANTHONY

TAVISTOCK PUBLICATIONS
London and New York

First published in 1986
by Tavistock Publications Ltd
11 New Fetter Lane,
London EC4P 4EE

Published in the USA by
Tavistock Publications
in association with Methuen, Inc.
29 West 35th Street,
New York NY 10001

Typeset by Hope Services, Abingdon
Printed in Great Britain by
Richard Clay (The Chaucer Press) Ltd,
Bungay, Suffolk

*British Library Cataloguing
in Publication Data*

Anthony, P.D.
The foundation of management.
—(Social science paperbacks; no. 324)
1. Industrial management—Great
Britain I. Title
658′.00941   HD70.G7

ISBN 0–422–61050–X
ISBN 0–422–78930–5 Pbk

*Library of Congress Cataloging-
in-Publication Data*

Anthony, Peter.
The foundation of management.
(Social science paperbacks; no. 324)
Bibliography: p.
Includes index.
1. Industrial management—Great
Britain. I. Title. II. Series: Social
science paperbacks; 324.
HD70.G7A58 1986   658′.00941
86–14427

ISBN 0–422–78930–5 (pbk.)

D
658.00941
ANT

For Catrin

Contents

Acknowledgements

I am grateful to the Senate of University College, Cardiff, for allowing me leave to undertake work for this book. I am also indebted to many friends, colleagues, and students, and particularly to Michael Reed, Tom Keenoy, and Nancy Harding for their helpful discussions and suggestions; it is no fault of theirs that errors remain.

I must thank Mrs Barbara Clargo and Mrs Mair Price for their patience and skill in typing this book. Finally, I am particularly grateful to my wife, Nia, for patiently reading the text and suggesting many improvements.

Introduction

The argument to be conducted here is that management, at least in Great Britain, has been engaged in a long retreat from responsibility for the control and direction of labour. This amounts to a serious indictment of managerial performance because management, by definition, is concerned with tasks that require it to engage and co-ordinate the services of subordinates so that the avoidance of these tasks amounts to an abrogation of its most fundamental role. If management is not accepting responsibility for the control of labour then it is not managing. I shall suggest not merely that this is the case, but that this refusal to manage has been carried out by persistent and deliberate strategies of avoidance accompanied by equally deliberate obfuscations which have had the effect of distracting attention from management's failure. The most consistent of these distractions is the provision of scapegoats as explanations for Britain's poor industrial performance, a tale of misfortune that lays blame at any door but management's.

The contention will be pursued and elaborated in four

different component parts. After dealing with two of the most persistent scapegoats, we shall look at the historical record of management's retreat, a process that will be described as a strategy of insulation. This strategy, it will be suggested, involves the search for an intermediary or buffer between labour and its direction. The strategy of insulation has involved three distinct attempts (to date) to find intermediaries. The first relied upon labour contractors, the second upon foremen or supervisors, the third upon a variety of functional specialists the most important of which have been the personnel managers. The conclusion of this account will suggest that each attempt fails but that failure is of no great consequence to management in pursuit of its grand design of self-protection; it can afford to sacrifice each of its surrogates as long as another is at hand.

The second part of the argument is that management's retreat has been the result, in part, of a misconceived theoretical explanation of its role and performance. There are two aspects of this misconception. The first is the result of an almost exclusive and certainly exaggerated concern with the economic and directive role of management. This exaggeration is associated with the second aspect, a preoccupation with the scientific or the technical function of management as against what Child (1969) distinguished as the legitimatory function of management. In order to make this point plainer, and to relate it more clearly to the general argument, I shall express that distinction by contrasting the technical with the governmental functions of management. I will suggest that management and its education (at least, once again, in Britain) have almost entirely ignored governmental functions and that that isolation is reflected in and related to the historical strategy of insulation. The abandonment of the governmental function of management is also a part of the main theme of the book; that is, the failure to give any systematic account or to engage in any consistent discussion of the nature and basis of managerial authority, to examine, in other words, the foundation of management.

The third perspective is concerned with the results of this failure. Within this, the first aspects are the industrial or occupational consequences. It is suggested that the passivity of much of the behavioural, motivational, and organizational design approaches to the achievement of improved employee performance stems from the failure to examine the fundamental relationship between management and labour in work. This has resulted in 'man mismanagement', a condition that has done more to produce lack of interest, low productivity, and industrial conflict than any assemblage of wreckers and dissident agitators could have achieved.

This is bad enough, but the problem may not be confined to the industrial and employment environment. Work, even when it is comparatively hard to come by, forms one of the most important sectors of our lives. It is important not only for economic reasons, but because of its moral and social significance as well. The point need not be stressed because it is familiar and obvious; what is not so obvious is that the decomposition of work is likely to have damaging consequences in the wider society. If the work of men and women is a significant part of their lives then the way they are directed in work is likely to be a significant influence on the way they live.

The most rigorous and severe representation of this argument descends from Marx by way of Gramsci and Marcuse. Capitalism is regarded as the dominant influence in contemporary society, controlling the processes of production and exchange to extract the maximum in surplus value to the advantage of the capitalist. The more original and straightforward accounts of the social dislocation caused by this ruthless but inevitable process of self-interested exploitation argued that it would increase both the misery and the numbers of the working class while necessarily organizing and educating it. The result would be equally inevitable: the working class would be given the need and the capacity to displace capitalist control so as to operate the productive process itself in its own interest. But the use of the future conditional has not been replaced by the present tense; capitalism remains untroubled, at least in those advanced industrial countries in which it was predicted that its troubles would begin.

The explanation for this state of affairs falls back upon the original analysis. It is because capitalism is more powerful even than it was first conceived to be that it remains in control. Capitalism's power is now seen to be more complex and to be manifested in more concrete and influential forms than in the 'mere' direction of the production process. Marxists have now recruited or influenced the whole range of social and critical studies to demonstrate the ways in which capitalist domination is achieved, in the hope, presumably, that the revelation of this domination behind the mask of consensus will itself do something to bring about its end. It is not our business to go into the various ways in which capitalist hegemony is exercised except in so far as it relates to our theme. In at least two respects, contemporary Marxism seeks to demonstrate the direct influence of our work upon our lives and outlook.

The first is by the recent development of the study of the labour process and the way in which it evolves. This has partly followed the publication of Braverman's *Labour and Monopoly Capitalism* in 1974. Braverman set out to demonstrate the ways in which capitalist control successively de-skilled and degraded the work of the skilled or semi-skilled worker. Subsequent critical responses to Braverman have, in the past, arisen from the degree of generalization in his account, the inadequacy of his definition of skill, his nostalgic exaggeration of the importance of craft work, and the insufficient attention he pays to management as the agent of the control of the labour process. The development of labour process studies by writers like Storey (1981, 1983), Littler (1983), and Paul Thompson (1983), although often critical, have been an extension of Braverman's work, provoked by its limitations rather than by an intention to refute it. Thompson says that the labour process perspective shows work to be 'not just something that a society organizes to meet social needs, or people carry out in order to survive' (Thompson 1983: 4), that a vital part of the labour process theory concerns the relationship between 'the physical forces and the social relations of production'. These writers, while respectfully acknowledging that the framework of this analysis was laid down by Marx, go on to say that it has not been adequately developed, has been allowed to lie fallow. Littler, therefore, criticizes the inadequacy of theory of exchange relationships for explaining what actually goes on in work: 'market models or notions of contract are inadequate conceptually to grasp the relations of subordination and domination governing the labour process' (Littler 1982: 32). Within the 'hidden abode of production', a great deal has to be done to achieve labour productivity (and surplus value) between the initial purchase of labour power and the final realization of the 'will, motivation and consciousness of the worker' (Edwards 1978). What has to be done includes the design of the production process, the control and co-ordination of labour, the achievement of at least a sufficient degree of consent and voluntary co-operation, the limitation of strategies of labour resistance, and the creation of a culture of work, no less. Most managers would be surprised at this job description of their activities but this is how they are seen, at least by Marxists. The historical dimension of this argument is that the process of technical production development, of mechanization itself, has been more directly related to the development of labour control (although, as we shall see, this account has been challenged by Gospel 1983).

The second direction taken by this argument about the influence of the work we have to do upon our lives, concerns managers as the agents. This also represents a revision (although entirely sympathetic) to earlier Marxist study and the work of Marx himself. Managers were given a rather shadowy existence in Marx, regarded as the functionaries of capital, doing what their masters bid them. This lack of attention encouraged and explained a tendency to leave managers out of any account of the labour movement and its institutions, to the extent that industrial relations, as an academic study rather than a practical activity, had little to do with management. This tendency has now been reversed and it is, again, on the left that the most fundamental reappraisal of management has been made. Managers are now seen as crucial to that process in which the purchase of labour is transformed into productive activity. They are now acknowledged to play their own unique and influential part in the subordination and control of labour and in the generation of a culture appropriate to the maintenance of the productive system.

It is odd that it is to the left that we should first turn to substantiate the claim that managers exert a considerable influence on our lives. One could expect that this conclusion would be so welcome to managers as to be loudly approved. But it does not appear to be so. There have been managerial theorists who have suggested that management, conducted according to the right principles, could be so influential as to provide a model for social organizations. Henry Ford proclaimed that message loudly, but it has not been widely broadcast and those who have relayed it have done so in an aside or, like F. W. Taylor (1911), have literally had the claim wrung from them under cross-examination. It is not a widely held view among management theorists; among practical managers, it is almost unheard. Why should there be so little support for the modest proposition that those who manage us in work exert considerable influence upon us within and beyond it? One possible explanation is that their influence depends upon their reticence, that to advertise their power would be to unmask it in precisely the way that their radical critics would do. Managers may prefer to be 'silent monitors' of our conduct and our attitudes. And if their influence in work is so obvious as to require no advertisement, the extension of that influence into our lives, to the degree that Marxists would describe it, is certainly not likely to be a matter for self-congratulatory notice lest it become a matter for public abatement. In this sense, the evidence and argument from the left may be more reliable than from the right. There would also seem to be some *a priori* reasons for believing that those who set out to control our work will, whether they wish it or not, influence our lives.

If that is so, there would be some purpose in enquiry as to the effect that management has upon our social and political relations. Further than that, it would be sensible to make this important activity a matter for study, so that managers could be helped to an understanding of what they did, so that they could do it the more effectively and exercise their great responsibility with more care for the rest of us. It would, in short, be no bad thing if management came to be regarded for what it is, a political activity and therefore the subject of philosophical and moral, as well as economic, attention. This attention has not been directed to management perhaps because it has been shunned by managers who might say, if they were to concern themselves with the question at all, that their influence is wider the less it is examined and that they are their own best arbiters of how it should be directed.

There seems to be a parallel between a lack of concern with the external influence of management upon society and the internal authority that it exercises. Both are governmental questions, matters of governance, the former much more deeply our general concern than the latter, which is indeed more a question of 'managerial prerogative'. The parallel between the external and internal aspects of managerial authority concerns its political character and the silence with which each is exercised. Storey (1983) is not alone in pointing out that managerial prerogatives have not been sufficiently analysed. I shall later argue, in response to Alasdair MacIntyre's (1981) trenchant criticisms of management, that it is not only a matter of public accountability that critical attention should be paid to the nature and exercise of management authority, but that it is a task made necessary in order to defend or facilitate the continuity of social relationships and moral intercourse. In this respect it would be no great exaggeration to say that, at least in MacIntyre's account, management has become the focus of the inherited arguments concerning the alienation and anomy brought about by capitalism. If management was the agent or functionary by which a reified capitalism brought about the destruction of an established order, and if the agent became rather more real and practical than the abstract forces it served, then management became the agent of destruction. And if, at the same time, the process was associated by philosophical develop- ments concerning the replacement of concepts of tradition, moral exchange, and virtuous conduct by a ruthless individualism and mechanistic utilitarianism, it is management, MacIntyre tells us, that has become the prime mover in achieving this change. If, in short, management is the villain of the piece, order cannot be restored without either removing the villain or reforming him.

Now the prospects for removing 'one of the central characters of our time' cannot be very real. What are the prospects for reform? No answer to that question can begin to emerge until we have begun to discuss the real nature of management's influence, its governmental activity, the nature of its authority and the way it is exercised, and the concealed assumptions that are made about management in the process of its education. What follows is an attempt to contribute to this discussion. It has two purposes and is, perhaps, directed at two audiences.

The first concern is with the internal relationships of management, within the confines of its enterprise, directed at subordinates, peers, and superordinates. In this context we are discussing matters related to managerial efficiency, the manner in which authority is exercised, and whether it would be better or worse for management to develop a critical awareness of its activities and relationships by developing, for example, more coherent and consistent policies toward labour and trade unions than it does. Thus, although the right to manage is an abstract claim, we will suggest that the extent to which it is well-founded and the manner of its justification are all practical matters that may have real consequences in terms of efficiency, productivity, and profit. To this extent, what follows is a management text although, it is to be hoped, of an unusual kind.

The second concern is with the external relationships of management, between those who control the enterprise and the society that surrounds it. This goes beyond an interest in the social responsibility of management, as one of the many claims that are made upon managerial attitudes, although social responsibility may be a derivative rather than a mark of the extent to which that relationship has been developed and understood. What I am setting out to examine here is the moral, the political, in MacIntyre's terms, the philosophical impli- cation of managerial outlook, behaviour, and influence. I am proposing to look at the consequences of management's exercise of its authority for the rest of us who are not simply its employees, but citizens of the world which it shapes almost as a by-product, an accidental extension of its relation with its subordinates. I am suggesting here that managerial authority is a most important matter in terms of social and political relationships, and that a preoccupation among those who manage or those who theorize about management 'merely' with internal questions of efficiency (which masks rather than exposes questions about authority) will necessarily confine any discussion of management to the partial and relatively insignificant.

The confinement of much of the contemporary discussion of management to questions concerning its techniques and its efficiency, its limitation to the confines of an economic sphere of activity, may, in fact, be a protective strategy for ensuring that it is left alone to get on with its quite limited and, for the most part, quite neutral, objectives of efficiency and utility while its unremarked external influence enables it to pursue them the more effectively, untrammelled by any political or moral constraint. This contention perhaps goes as far as any other to explain why a question concerning the social and political significance of management should appear at first sight to be so strange and to have been, hitherto, largely unexamined.

I shall end with the suggestion that this state of affairs will continue as long as management is seen as engaged in an exclusively economic context, and also with the modest proposal that managerial organizations, once understood to be primarily communities (albeit concerned with economic ends), can then take their place within the wider social and moral environment so that their inhabitants can be more readily subject to social and moral regulation. Two advantages will be claimed for this perspective. First, that it provides a framework in which it may be possible to address the almost traditional problems of alienation in industrial societies, by placing the controllers of that society within, rather than outside, the overall social network. Second, that it is not only better (in the prospect it offers for the solution of problems that otherwise may appear to be intractable); it is also more real.

1
Scapegoats

There is little discussion of managerial incompetence above the level of the shop floor in this country. There are several likely explanations, apart from the unlikely one that it is never a problem that requires attention. Those most concerned with it, consultants and academic analysts of management performance, are the clients of management, and their discussions, although no doubt trenchant, are likely to be conducted behind closed doors. Those most knowledgeable, the managers themselves, are employees, for the most part, of organizations for whom loyalty is regarded as co-extensive with employment. Those most ostensibly critical of management, the trade unions, have two reasons for discretion: criticism of managerial performance implies an interest in and responsibility for the direction of the enterprise's affairs that British trade unions have traditionally eschewed; the collective bargaining relationship narrowly defines the area of joint discussion and, by mutual agreement, consigns much that is important to silence. The consequence is like the result of a conspiracy although, in this case, there may be no conspirators. Even when foremen maintain that their managers knew that their subordinates regularly slept on the night-shift, that disturbance of the sleepers would have required managerial authority, and that without it they were powerless, a tribunal sympathetically exonerates management and supports the dismissal of the foremen.

If, for whatever reasons, management is largely exempted from criticism for poor performance and if the performance of British industry is judged to be bad then other explanations must be advanced. I am going to suggest that the two most frequent explanations are inadequate, that they serve as screens to continue to protect management from embarrassing examination, that the first of them is a scapegoat in the selection of which management has had some responsibility, and that the second is merely an academic fashion. The first of them is the scapegoat of industrial relations, the second is the myth of British culture. We shall deal with each in turn, the first of them more briefly because it is, at the present time, less credible.

'Bad News', the results of research carried out by the Glasgow Media Group (1976), established beyond reasonable doubt that newspapers, television, and radio news shared a predilection to exaggerate or emphasize the severity of industrial disputes and their consequences. It has also been noticeable that the focus of media attention has moved to whatever industrial sector was currently active in terms of the generation of disputes, in order to sustain the view that poor industrial relations in Britain as a whole explained poor British economic performance. Thus, in the 1950s and 1960s, when the majority of British strikes took place in the coal-mining industry, hardly a day seemed to pass without sorrowful attention being paid to the latest dispute and its serious consequences. In the late 1960s, as the incidence of coal-mining strikes dwindled almost to vanishing point (as the result of a strategic change in pay structure), attention shifted to the engineering industry and to the motor manufacturing section especially. The Donovan Commission, which reported in 1968, was criticized, significantly from our perspective, for its preoccupation with the British engineering industry and its tendency to generalize, both in terms of analysis and recommendations, from that singular but important sector to the whole of industry. After a brief but dramatic return to the forefront by the coal industry in 1972 and 1974, the number and severity of disputes dwindled until in 1982 it was that most traditionally peaceful area, the public sector, that captured media attention in the 'winter of discontent'. The regicidal resonance of that phrase and the frightening images of hospital patients who, untreated, might die to remain unburied, continued to convince us that industrial relations was at the heart of the British disease, a condition that merited continual legislative treatment.

We are not engaged here in an advertisement for British industrial relations. However, it certainly deserves no general condemnation. Anyone informed upon the subject is likely to agree that the causes of an industry's strike pattern are likely to be highly specific and the explanations of a particular dispute to be highly complex. Generalizations from such patterns or such incidents to a diagnosis of the faults of the British economy and to overall presumptions for a remedy are likely to be unreliable and irrelevant. This is particularly the case when a cursory analysis of dispute statistics usually reveals an overwhelming picture of peace in which most employees in most places of employment rarely experience industrial disputes. The image of strike-proneness falsely attributed to British industry in general is derived from a relatively high incidence of disputes in very large units of employment confined to particular industries.

There is no doubt that the image is exaggerated. Keenoy, taking the figures of working days lost through strikes as a percentage of potential working time, tells us that the absolute amount of working time lost between 1946 and 1973 was 0.07 per cent. 'What this means – if the losses are spaced evenly throughout the working population – is that every employee loses 20.16 seconds in an 8-hour day through strikes' (Keenoy 1985: 176–77). And, as he reminds us, the comparisons made by Hyman show that in 1970 when strikes reached a new post-war high point at 10 million working days lost that figure represented 50 per cent of the losses due to industrial accidents, 5 per cent of the losses due to unemployment, and 3.3 per cent of losses due to certified sickness (Hyman 1972).

But managers will not be the first to tell us that British indusry does not deserve the reputation it has acquired in industrial relations. Strikes are not entirely unwelcome to managers, and in some circumstances they are particularly useful. The most extreme case is that in which strikes are alleged to have been caused by managers. Such claims have indeed been made in the motor industry – that when order books are empty and the delivery parks are full, a temporary shut-down without attendant lay-off costs will be sufficiently attractive to make management pursue a singularly reckless course in industrial relations.

The more usual response to industrial dispute is to regard it as an area in which all events are acts of God so that no responsibility can be attributed to management for what occurs in it. Thus, industrial relations, like the weather for farmers, is at once an explanation for disaster and for a shortfall from perfection. Either in company reports and accounts or in the self-justifications of a particular manager, industrial relations is an explanation for what might have been and why it is not. Rarely, it is seen for what it is by senior managers: a scapegoat. Mr Shepherd, sometime production director of the National Coal Board, used to berate colliery managers by telling them, on his arrival in his high office, some seventy 'ITM' pits had been identified and that the number had subsequently been reduced to four, of which two were probably, in his view, 'genuinely ITM' pits. The bravest of his audiences would, sooner or later, ask what was meant by 'ITM'. Mr Shepherd would reply that he meant 'It's the Men' pits, where managers constantly blamed labour relations for shortfalls in efficiency, productivity, or profit. He would then announce that it was his mission to ensure that responsibility for these matters should lie where it belonged, with management.

In the 1980s, at a time of high unemployment when the incidence of disputes has fallen to a low level, the industrial relations scapegoat is not so often used, but we shall no doubt hear more of it when times improve. In the meantime a much more general, potent, and dangerous scapegoat has been presented: no less than the cultural and historic incapacity of the British for work.

What follows is an attempt to give an account of this case as it has been presented in its most lucid and coherent form, by Professor Martin J. Wiener (1981). This will be followed by a critical examination of that case. The excuse for this lengthy aside is twofold. In the first place, Professor Wiener's argument has achieved considerable influence, popularized by two successive Monday hours of prime television time, given the approval and blessing of authorities as widely dispersed as Professor Ralf Dahrendorf, Mr Neil Kinnock, and Mr Enoch Powell, awarded the American Historical Association Prize for British History, and described by *New Society* as having 'become part of the received wisdom in interpreting recent British history and our prospects for the future' (*New Society* 17 November, 1983: 274). It is this received wisdom that I shall attempt to reduce, to use Profesor Wiener's precise words, to 'the level of general bullshit' (*New Society* 17 November, 1983: 275). The second reason for this exercise, apart from a necessary attempt to correct error as being valuable in itself, is that the error is currently the most powerful reason for not examining the culpability of management for whatever are the deficiencies in our condition. So, while we are ultimately concerned with management and what is wrong with it, it is first necessary to remove an obstacle to that objective.

In *English Culture and the Decline of the Industrial Spirit, 1850–1980* (1981) Professor Wiener tells us that

'for a long time, the English have not felt comfortable with "progress". As one social analyst* has perceived, "progress" is a word that in England has come to possess a curiously ambiguous emotive power. "It connotes tendencies that we accept, even, formally approve, yet of which we are privately suspicious" [quoting from Allison]. It is an historic irony that the nation that gave birth to the industrial revolution, and exported it throughout the world, should have become embarrassed at the measure of its success. The English nation even became ill at ease enough with its prodigal progeny to deny its legitimacy by adopting a conception of Englishmen that virtually excluded industrialism.'

(Wiener 1981: 5)

Britain came to suspect material and technological development and industrialism and the suspicion pervaded education. The

---

* He turns out to be Lincoln Allison, writing in *New Society* on 16 February, 1978, the same analyst who was to conduct an uncritical discussion with Wiener in *New Society* on 17 November, 1983, after the publication of Wiener's book.

values of growth and technical innovation gave way to the 'contrary ideals' of tranquility, closeness to the past, non-materialism, the values of a rural idyll. In this way a conflict of values was set up, between progress and nostalgia, between material growth and moral stability.

In pursuit of this thesis Professor Wiener takes help from wherever he can get it. From the new left he cites Perry Anderson and Tom Nairn, arguing that industrialization took place in Britain while the aristocracy was becoming stronger and richer, that there was no antagonism between the old autocracy and the new bourgeoisie, that even if both classes were capitalist they were 'not capitalist in the same way', that aristocratic capitalism was *rentier* not entrepreneurial; 'the *rentier* aristocracy succeeded in maintaining a cultural hegemony and consequently . . . . In reshaping the industrial bourgeoisie in its own image' (Wiener 1981: 8). The consequence was a merger rather than a conquest, a marriage rather than a rape, the civilizing of the bourgeoisie. The product was 'a new dominant bourgeois culture bearing the imprint of the old aristocracy' and the practical result is to be found in 'new towns and green belts, the love of gardening, even as wariness of most modern architecture . . . [and] persistent economic retardation' (1981: 10).

In the re-cast British life of the second half of the nineteenth century, public schools became central to the process of social consolidation. They produced a new ethos held by a homogeneous and cohesive élite that shared the same educational outlook and values that represented an adaptation by the landed ruling class but also 'a crucial rebuff for the social revolution begun by industrialization' (Wiener 1981: 12). The aristocracy prolonged its own reign, power was yielded in return for time and for the acceptance of many of the aristocratic values by the members of the new élite. Wiener acknowledges that individual aristocrats might have been 'development minded' and interested in industrial enterprise but says that 'yet one can accept the economic vitality of the landed élite and still argue for their long-run inhibiting effect on the national economy' (1981: 173–74). (How one can accept this remains unclear.) Thus the gentry preserved their predominance without abandoning their distinctive values and style of life to which the new businessman and industrialist came to aspire. Wiener cites a passage from Samuel Smiles's *Self-Help* on 'the character of a true gentleman' in order to establish the conclusion that gentility was, for Smiles, 'the ultimate crown to be worn by those who had helped themselves' (1981: 174).

Wiener goes on to examine the growth of the professions and the universities in order to sustain and develop his argument. The growth of the modern professions 'bolstered the emerging cultural containment of industrial capitalism' (Wiener 1981: 15), and the professions were maintained by their nurseries, the public schools, the anti-scientific bias of which was extended by the values of the older universities, which 'insulated the sons of older élites against contact with industry' and 'drew sons of industrial and commercial families away from the occupations of their fathers' (1981: 24). So, businessmen sought to act like educated gentlemen, and, as educated gentlemen (or would-be gentlemen) entered business, economic behaviour altered. 'The dedication to work, the drive for profit, and the readiness to strike out on new paths in its pursuit waned' (1981: 24).

The watershed of British industrial and economic values was the Great Exhibition of 1851, the 'high-water mark of educated opinion's enthusiasm for industrial capitalism (Wiener 1981: 28). After that it was downhill 'toward the domestication of the industrial revolution (1981: 30). And worse was to follow. Wiener cites J. S. Mill, Dickens, Arnold, and Ruskin as representing a conservative revolution in mid- and late-Victorian England. The upper, middle, and professional classes developed a culture and a world view that was characterized by 'outward acceptance of modernity without inner conviction' (1981: 40). By the 1870s the past, instead of being used to make innovation palatable, was being valued for its own sake. Criticism of cities and the kind of life that was lived in them became more and more common. Wiener traces the predominance of such anti-urban values in literature and in architecture.

In literature the tale descends from 'country writing', the eulogizing of rural England with the squire as its central character, through Thomas Hardy and Richard Jefferies to Kipling, who represents, writing from his country home in Sussex, the apotheosis of respect for a rural past, 'the product of a self-conscious quest for the national identity' (Wiener 1981: 57). The literary lineage ends with references to Hewlett, Rupert Brooke, Ernest Rhys, E. V. Lucas, Edward Hutton, and Flecker.

The architectural lineage is even stranger. The story begins with the Gothic revival and the simultaneous rise of preservationism and continues down to Norman Shaw, Voysey, and nostalgia for old England and the middle ages. Wiener comments, not without reason, that preservationism implies, first 'a loss of confidence in the creative powers of one's contemporaries and an elevation of the past over the present; and second, a highly critical view of industrial capitalism and its "materialistic" ethos' (1981: 69).

Wiener brings this part of the discussion together with the main theme of the work with the statement that 'by now it should seem clear to the reader that the vision of a tranquilly rustic and traditional national way of life permeated English life and that any understanding of British economic development must take account of that fact' (1981: 81). But this is not all. He distinguishes between two groups of 'new' businessmen, the one based on commerce and finance, operating in the city, the other on manufacturing and based in the north. The banking system virtually withdrew from industry largely because of the greater profitability of the developing world economy but also as a result of the social separation 'that already existed between the worlds of finance and industry, and the contemporaneous entrenchment of anti-industrial sentiments in the financial and professional classes (1981: 129).

All things thus conspire to produce an English contempt, if not for the useful, then for the profitable and industrial. Education continues the story to the present day. Universities are roads out of, not in to, industry. Engineering is regarded with contempt, 'the engineer's low status is at the heart of our problem' (Wiener 1981: 135). The public schools continued to direct their best pupils away from industry while an increasing number of highly placed industrial managers were the products of public schools. Wiener grants that an increasing proportion of the output of the public schools goes into business but that is the result of education for status, not for industry. 'More and more in the twentieth century, the higher echelons of the larger businesses were dominated by men whose standards had been formed in the gentlemanly mould' (1981: 138–39). The marked prejudice against production and marketing continued but with an added qualification. Production could be valued 'if it were separated from questions of utility, and treated as a pure technical problem' (1981: 141). This was precisely the case at Rolls-Royce where the 'pure engineering' ethos and 'the disdain of the gentleman for the descent into the market place was reproduced, and obsession with production legitimized. The price was eventual bankruptcy in 1971' (1981: 141). Wiener also acknowledges that 'the life of finance was readily reconcilable with the gentry ideal' (1981: 145).

He concludes that the current de-industrialization of Britain has been preceded by a century of psychological and intellectual de-industrialization.

Wiener's argument, of which this is an inadequate summary, like all ingredients of received wisdom or explanatory myth, has several merits. It is attractively simple and easy to understand, at least in the absence of close analysis. It has, as an argument, considerable merit and a great deal of evidence to support several of its separate assertions. It falls on sympathetic ears: the aristocracy and its values has few determined friends and is sufficiently remote from the experience of most of us to be a safe matter for generalization, if not of undetected error. Best of all, while it leaves us with a satisfying feeling of moral outrage, it leaves us with nothing to do and little or no sense of responsibility for our deplorable condition. The gentrification argument produces a satisfactory scapegoat and distracts our attention from what would otherwise be a much more painful process of self-analysis and correction. But it will not do, and before we get to necessary correction we must first attempt to remove this attractive obstacle to it.

First, as to the alleged preponderance of traditional, English, aristocratic values. Now it may be perfectly clear, seen from Wiener's Rice University, USA, what these values are but, from nearer at hand, things seem a bit more confused. Aristocratic money has long been acknowledged to be a necessary ingredient in the industrial revolution. Aristocratic outlooks have often been seen to encompass a rapacious self-interest. Habbakuk is quoted as affirming that the aristocracy acquires land to enjoy it rather than to make money out of it, but the eighteenth century agricultural innovations of Townshend and Young were widely imitated to the great advantage of the landowners in establishing an agricultural industry of great efficiency and profitability. One of the most significant landscaping features of the eighteenth century is the ha-ha, which enabled the productive home farm to come right up to the front terrace without disturbance of the household on the one hand and the milk yield on the other. The recruitment of Samuel Smiles's advertisement for the character of a gentleman is also unconvincing. Smiles, says Wiener, persuades people to admire a new ideal, that of the aristocratic values of cultivated style, leisure, and political service rather than zeal for work and inventiveness. But this is entirely the opposite of Smiles's intention and of his actual argument. He distinguishes the English aristocracy particularly from the French by virtue of the English gentry's characteristic energy and inventiveness. Gentlemanliness, for Smiles, is expressed in moral virtue, in good sense, good principles, obedience to conscience, integrity, industry, civility, and kindness. These sternly Protestant virtues are precisely what keeps the English aristocracy and, by its example, the English people from the decadent ways of the French. In fact, says Smiles, it is only these gentlemanly qualities that enable the English aristocracy to overcome the grave disadvantages, and temptations to sloth, of wealth, rank, intellect, and ability. By commending the advantages of the character of a gentleman, Smiles's position rebuts rather than supports the gentrification argument as it is advanced by Wiener. Smiles is on the other side, as, in other respects, Wiener acknowledges.

The argument concerning education is in some ways the most persuasive. This is partly because of the confused influences exerted by the educators (particularly in the universities) and the complex relationships between them and their changing environment. An admirable account of this confusion is to be found in Rothblatt's *The Revolution of the Dons* (1981) – but not much of this subtle complexity is transmitted in Wiener's account. And yet, upon examination, some concealed confusions do begin to appear. The products of the public schools are headed away from business and industry as the result of the schools' aristocratic contempt for the useful (a jibe that was not even true of the Greeks upon whom the public school ethos was supposedly modelled). But, alternatively, business and industry come to be dominated by the effete values of the aristocracy as more and more public school products get into business and management. Either education ignores business (which supports the gentrification thesis) or business is dominated by an educated élite (which supports the gentrification thesis). The universities are similarly accused of ignoring business values and of contributing to the development of engineering, the professions, science, or the City at the expense of manufacturing industry. The argument, thus, not only generalizes too greatly about whatever is its current subject, it is also gravely ambiguous about that subject, which is sometimes presented as business, sometimes capital enterprise, sometimes industry, sometimes productive manufacturing. By dexterously manipulating both the subject (education, for example) and the object ('business' or 'industry') all evidence and argument can be pressed to the unavoidable conclusion that 'gentrification' has been our ruination.

The strategy is revealed at its most effective in the more detailed argument concerning English literature and English architecture, effective at least until a little more attention is given to them.

Wiener cites, to some effect, the anti-industrial literary attack pressed home by Dickens, Arnold, and Ruskin, establishing a tradition carried on by Hardy, Jefferies, Watson, Noyes, Newbolt, and Austin. Perhaps we may be forgiven for sticking to the better-known members of this romantic alliance. It is true that there are elements of a literary and intellectual reaction to industrialization in England, that it is interesting and deserves, and has received, critical analysis. It is also true that this reaction to forces that appeared shattering and dangerous concerned their effects on class relationships, moral order, and social stability and that the element in the reaction that was the most straightforwardly negative was entirely unsuccessful, was without influence, and was dismissed as eccentric. If Ruskin can be regarded as the most forthright and consistent of the critics of capitalist industrialization, it is certainly true that he was dismissed as a 'mad governess', that his editor, W. M. Thackeray, was 'forced' to drop his attacks from the Cornhill Magazine, that his books of social criticism did not sell. Ruskin saw himself, correctly, as an outsider, snapping at the heels of an enormously powerful economic orthodoxy entrenched in the City and in Manchester, an invention of the British, propped up by an unassailable and equally British science of political economy, the authority of which was established as being beyond criticism. This is nearer the truth of the critical literary tradition. Wiener is trying to make the critical fringe (dismissed by its contemporaries as lunatic) look like the orthodoxy that it was attacking while he steadfastly refuses to recognize orthodoxy's existence. Some of the literary representatives cited as examples of the critical tradition are also of questionable value to the argument. Is it right to see Thomas Hardy as representing the triumph of the values of rural old England, or is Hardy more properly to be understood as recording those values for a generation that will never know them again, as harvest home and the wassailers give way to the steam traction engine and the depopulated land? And Kipling, cited as the celebrant of old England (with reference to one poem and two stories), could more properly be regarded as the English writer most usually concerned with work, with competence (in engineers, in soldiers, or in journalists), and with practical good sense.

Architecture, says Wiener, is 'the myth made tangible' (Wiener 1981: 64). A myth indeed, as it turns out. His account begins with the nineteenth-century revival of the Gothic style but he has to acknowledge that the revival failed because it was taken over by the enemy in Manchester and Bradford. The failure was, of course, also acknowledged by two of its proponents, Ruskin and Pugin, who saw that the revival failed to achieve the prominence of Christian values over those of functionalist capitalism, proving, if anything, the opposite of the case that Wiener seeks to establish. English architecture, according to Wiener, following the Gothic's failure, turned to the Arts and Crafts Movement with Voysey and Norman Shaw, turned to old England, the invocation of the past in place of the present. This is true, up to a point, but it begs several questions. The Arts and Crafts Movement was generally regarded as idiosyncratic, a by-way irrelevant to, and swamped by, the modernist functionalism which begat our high-rise flats and tower blocks. Oddly, for reasons quite different from those advanced by Wiener, the Movement may yet turn out to have been of more significance than modernism. It is now acknowledged in some quarters to have influenced British suburban housing, which can be claimed to have produced the most efficient, cost-effective form of housing for a modestly affluent industrial population.

Together, the arguments from literature and from architecture are misdirected in detail and unreliable in conclusion. They share a presupposition with a fringe of irrelevance (although, to the extent that they contain *post hoc* truths they open up yet another criticism of Wiener – what if they were right all along?). They ignore the vast and overwhelming orthodoxy of British nineteenth- and twentieth-century theory and practice. They ignore the point that was made by Ruskin, Leavis, and modern Marxists, that the values of business, progress, and competition are established, that the criticism is of a vast and exclusive consensus.

The most dangerous aspect of Wiener's whole argument is what makes it the most attractive and convincing. While the values of the aristocracy are defined vaguely so is the identity of the alternative value system that the aristocracy is claimed to have defeated. The alternative modern, presumably preferable, ethos is variously titled, as we have seen, so that Wiener can shift his attack, when it breaks down, from one object to another without acknowledging that there has been a change. Thus the distinction between two groups of businessmen, the one active in commerce, the other in manufacturing. This distinction is of great utility in maintaining, for example, the criticism of education for directing its products to the City rather than to industry and in insisting that finance capital (judged from a radical perspective to be the true ringmaster of all industrial undertakings) somehow represents the unchanging romantic tenacity of the old traditional order. The confusions enable Wiener to claim that the introduction of engineering into the curricula of British universities is irrelevant to the gentrification argument or even that it actually establishes that argument's validity. Thus the educational system is accused of reflecting society's prejudice against marketing, production, and engineering. Engineering, he tells us, is regarded with contempt, vocational studies have low status, 'the engineer's low status is at the heart of our problem' (Wiener 1981: 135). But, 'there was one way that production could be valued: if it were separated from questions of utility and treated as a purely technical problem' (Wiener 1981: 141), which is why we got into the Rolls-Royce impasse. We cannot win this argument, it seems, unless perhaps we send for the accountants and ask them to exercise the most stringent financial control over our engagement in treating purely technical problems. But Wiener will no doubt then tell us that we are demonstrating our aristocratic contempt for production by generating the old gentrified values enshrined in the professions.

Finally, there is throughout all this a steadfast refusal to evaluate the evidence from any fixed and recognizable standpoint, either theoretical or moral. Thus *The Engineer* is quoted for its comment in 1911 that 'there are fair and unfair ways of diminishing labour costs. . . . We do not hesitate to say that Taylorism is inhuman' (Wiener 1981: 43). There you are, says Wiener, a typical English addiction to anti-industrial values. Even English economists, like Marshall and Keynes, are said to have taken a 'lofty view' of the world of business for having suggested that material improvements were important because they contributed to human well-being rather than being ends in themselves. But what if *The Engineer* and the economists were right? The reader gets the impression that a critic of the cholera outbreaks of the 1840s, or of the deaths at Peterloo, or of the unemployment of the 1930s or the 1980s, or any of the less attractive accompaniments of capitalist industrialization, would be cited for revealing evidence of addiction to aristocratic values and of the influence of gentrification.

Perhaps we should remember that the alternative view, of a prevailing capitalist hegemony, is as unlikely as the English romantic orthodoxy that Wiener sets against it. Perhaps we should settle for the recognition that alternative values to those of the hegemony survive and that this survival is a flickering recollection picked up in some traditions, reflected in the popularity of chocolate boxes with pictures of roses round the door. Perhaps this English myth is just as real as the German fondness for a traditional forest-dwelling past and the American tradition of the frontier, long dead. The reality of that myth is what gives Wiener's argument some credibility, but it is a credibility as dangerous as the myth upon which it rests. Apart from the inaccuracy of Wiener's case as an explanation for the poor performance of the British economy, the case is dangerously irrelevant. There is no practical progress to come from attacking a convenient scapegoat and in demanding that, in some unspecified way, our values have to change. The aristocracy is both remote and convenient; it causes us no discomfort to be told that it should be controlled, reformed, or, if necessary, executed.

The irrelevance and invalidity of the argument about gentrification would be of no great concern if its attraction did not include the excuse it provides for refusing to attend to our real problems. The attribution of their causes to industrial disputes and to gentrification avoids the necessity of making practical and painful changes. It prevents us, in particular, from attending to that group that has clearest responsibility for the direction of production of goals and services – management. While it is in the interest of management to advance strikes and trade union behaviour as scapegoats, deliberately chosen to carry our sins, the gentrification argument cannot be seen as a protective strategy engaged in by managers. They may be grateful to it but it is not theirs. They may, in fact, turn out to be not so much the innocent victims as the undeserving beneficiaries of the class war conducted on an intellectual plane.

They must not be allowed to escape. There are several good reasons for focusing upon managers as the most likely cause of our present troubles. First among them is the claim they make themselves to hold responsibility for the direction of resources in the pursuit of economic objectives. They exercise, if not a right, then certainly a claim to responsibility. The claim has considerable truth because responsibility is not only claimed, it is exercised. The controlling of business and industrial affairs is what they do, it is the usual activity of managers. There is, therefore, an immediate rather than a remote relationship between managers and economic performance. The relationship is reinforced by a large degree of public support. One way and another, considerable resources are devoted to management, not as a charitable act but because of that perceived relationship to economic goals and their achievement. Not only are managers paid large salaries for work that is deemed to be productive and useful but considerable sums are devoted by their organizations to their selection, training, and development, while the public makes its contribution by financing, at least in part, prestigious business schools in the sector of higher education.

The immediacy of managerial responsibility for economic performance is a case that does not need to be laboured. But behind that practical relationship is a more obscure layer of responsibility. The most extreme case for uncovering it was made by James Burnham in *The Managerial Revolution* (1941). The passage that follows neatly illustrates both the extent of his claim for management and its relationship to the more humdrum and practical level of managerial responsibility. Burnham is arguing that the managers or bureaucrats are about to become the ruling class, that they can no longer be seen merely as managers in the technical or practical sense:

'The managers are certainly concerned directly in production: indeed, the development of modern industry places them in the *key* positions of production even *before* the transition to managerial society takes place. Before the managerial structure is consolidated, the managers function throughout enterprise, both private and governmental. With the consolidation of the managerial structure, which includes the state monopoly of all important enterprise, the position of the managers is assured. To a large extent . . . the managers and the bureaucrats fuse into a single class with a united interest. Far from being incapable of constituting a ruling class, the managers, by the very conditions of modern technology and contemporary institutional evolution, would have a hard time avoiding rule.'

(Burnham 1941: 266)

Burnham argued that the managers would constitute themselves into a ruling class, that they would exercise

'control over the instruments of production and gain preference in the distribution of the products, not directly, through property rights vested in them as individuals, but indirectly, through their control of the state which in turn will own and control the instruments of production.'

(Burnham 1941: 69)

The less extreme version of the case for managerial power exercised beyond the level of its practical and productive functions comes down from Berle and Means who argued that, because of the dispersion and complexity of stockholding among modern corporations, ownership had been replaced by management as the controller of organizations, that there had been a divorce between ownership and control (Berle and Means 1932). Other statements of the managerialist argument suggest that management has replaced ownership in terms of the exercise of authority, that management is crucial in the control of enterprises as 'imperatively coordinated associations' (Dahrendorf, 1959). All these various statements that stress the enhanced importance of management in social affairs and beyond the confines of the place of work have been criticized. The grounds for the criticism concerns empirical justification and lack of definition; the motive for the criticism may be related to the view that managerialism is associated with the position that ownership's replacement by management is a manifestation of the development of a 'post-capitalist' society, which, if it were to be conceded, would refute the predictive analysis of Marx. It is not our business either to describe or to adjudicate in this debate. It is sufficient for us to observe that while the more extreme statements of the case for transcendent managerial power have been challenged, there is no qualification to the view that management is a potent influence both inside the enterprise and beyond it.

There are several ways in which this influence is exercised. If the majority of the population is employed or is directly dependent upon those who are employed then those who exercise authority over the hours of employment are likely to exert considerable influence upon behaviour. Managers are also likely to extend the influence of their enterprise beyond its confines in at least two directions. First, they will, in order to promote the greater productive effort of their workers, seek to control or adjust the way in which their workers live. This extra-mural influence can extend from the benign and enlightened attempt to educate and reform that has characterized employers from Robert Owen and Titus Salt to Mond to the more overt moral espionage system of Henry Ford. Second, they will attempt to influence the attitudes and behaviour of the public at large. Such attempts range from the innocent advertising of goods, to the production of an image of a commendable and trustworthy company, and the manipulation of a context of opinion judged to be favourable for the company's product. The Tobacco Advisory Council's campaign, 'Speaking up for Smokers', might serve as an example. The more general and diffuse level at which managers exert influence is advertised more on the left than the right. It concerns the political and social influence of managers as the necessary intermediaries between capital and labour, which is increasingly a question debated by labour process theorists, as we shall see, and, finally, it concerns the managerial contribution to the construction and maintenance of hegemony. Our own concern in the remainder of this discussion is not how managers exercise this influence, which would be a dauntingly difficult descriptive task, but how they justify their influence. We are concerned, in short, with the basis of managerial authority.

The explanation for this concern is that influence justified by authority is likely to be judged to be legitimate by those over whom it is exercised and is therefore likely to be effective. If management influence is widespread, as most of us would concede it to be, then its authority is also a political question. That question becomes the more urgent if, as Drucker said:

> 'Managerial power today is illegitimate power. It is in no way based upon a fundamental principle accepted by society as a legitimate basis of power. It is not controlled by such a principle or limited by it. And it is responsible to no one.'
>
> (Drucker 1965: 75)

If this is true then management's lack of concern with the basis of its own authority is likely to have two consequences, each serious enough to demand attention. The first is that its authority will be inefficiently exercised in its internal relationship. The second is that it will be irresponsibly exercised in both its internal and external relationships.

2

Managerial authority, control, and co-operation

One of the difficulties to be encountered before discussing the foundation of management is to determine what is management. It would be dispiriting and unproductive to deal with this problem by a lengthy examination of definitions of the managerial function and I shall avoid it, but the difficulty is a real one and cannot be sidestepped. It is real in the sense that many managers are unsure of their claim to that title. A works chief engineer, for example, will certainly regard himself as a manager but will say that he used to be an engineer. Many of his subordinate staff will see themselves as engineers rather than managers. IBM makes a clear distinction between its managerial and professional staff. The NHS distinguishes between administrative and unit managers, and its most influential and respected employees, the medical staff, see themselves as neither although their influence and status is envied by both.

A more important difficulty concerns the specialization and

differentiation to which tasks widely acknowledged to be managerial have been subjected. Management can include anything from the wide and general direction of affairs at board level to the specific, narrow, and specialized responsibility for computer services or quality control. In the latter respect, management can be seen to have a highly technical and specialized content related to the kind of responsibility under-taken by the works engineers. Some managers, then, are seen as engaged in something very like a professional kind of task, judged by their expertise in applying specialized knowledge and techniques. The need for managerial specialism has grown and has been accompanied by the proliferation of techniques of data collection, analysis, and planning. Both processes have contributed to the belief that management is usually concerned with precise knowledge and the application of highly specialized skills. The belief has been further encouraged by the claim that, while general management is something of a mystery, the managerial techniques required by the growing number of specialists can be taught and applied.

We shall have more to say about the distinction between general and specialized management and about the associated difference between governmental and technical aspects of management. They are inseparable aspects of any manager's job but we are not going to be primarily concerned with managerial specialists. Our concern is with line managers. The phrase 'line managers' is, of course, untidy and ambiguous. Line responsibility is usually associated with production but in many organizations the physical production process may not have the same importance or managerial centrality as, say, in motor manufacturing or mining. So let us be more precise. We are primarily concerned with that part of management that is concerned in the control and co-ordination of subordinate labour. We are not, therefore, going to have a lot to say about financial management except as an influence or constraint upon management in the sense that we have delineated it. Our concern is with line or with general management in so far as it is normally exercised through subordinate labour. We shall also be attentive to those specialized aspects of management that are engaged in the provision of assistance and advice to 'line' management in its control and co-ordination of labour.

In terms of the proliferation of managerial specialisms with which we began this might seem to be an overly narrow restriction of the subject matter. It is not so. In the first place, *all* management, even of the most specialist kind in which the technical element is great, is, by definition, concerned in the achievement of its own objectives through the co-ordination and control of subordinate labour. Management, as Child (1969) tells us, requires action through other people. The aspect of management with which we are concerned is fundamental to all management. Our chief works engineer is a manager and no longer an engineer, despite the continuing engineering content of his job, because he must work through subordinates, albeit that most of them may be engineers. This discussion is about labour control but it is not about labour management or personnel management in the narrow, functional, and specialized sense in which those terms are usually employed. It is about the element of labour management and control that is the essential characteristic of all managerial jobs. Industrial relations and personnel management specialists are relevant to the discussion to the extent that they contribute to managerial effectiveness in labour control.

The means by which labour control is achieved are not simple, although, in the earlier stages of industrialization, they may have appeared to be so. The accounts given by Engels, Gaskell, and nineteenth-century moralists of poverty, danger, and the exercise of coercive control are familiar. The means by which the employer exercised control over his work force emanated from unemployment, the fear of destitution, the exercise of unbridled power, the absence or weakness of collective organization among employees, and the reinforcement of the employers' power by the law. Such a catalogue of strength would suggest an imbalance of power in favour of the employer so overwhelming as to make any additions or refinements quite unnecessary. It is a measure of the inadequacy of employment control based upon coercion that employers searched in various directions for reinforcement and alternatives.

It has been argued that the deliberate pursuit of three grand strategies was necessary to supplement the power of the employer. The first was mechanization itself, introduced not only as a means to higher productivity and profit, but as an essential means of labour control. Thus Berg argues that the power loom

> 'was profitable only for certain fabrics. . . . It was quite clear to many that the productivity of the power loom was not its greatest asset. Consistent production time, and control and supervision over manufacturing processes in the factory were rather its more powerful attractions to the manufacturer.'
>
> (Berg 1980: 241–42)

She quotes the Bolton Committee of Manufacturers and Weavers: 'The chief advantage of power looms is the facility of executing a quantity of work under more immediate control and management, and the prevention of embezzlement, and not in the reduced cost of production' (Berg 1980: 242). The argument for the pursuit of a policy of mechanization with control as its main objective has been criticized. Howard Gospel suggests that the dichotomy of efficiency and control as the main aims of factory development is too simple. The relationship between factory discipline and employer control is questionable, he says, if only because of the extent to which the employer appeared to have avoided rather than pursued control by the widespread use of the internal labour contracting system (Gospel 1983). A related argument suggests that mechanization, the development of the division of labour, and the associated hierarchical organization of labour and supervision contributed to breaking up the unity of workers and the cohesion of any resistance they might be able to offer to employers. The more extensive use of machinery meant, says Berg, that

> 'the designing and direction of the work passed away from the hands of the workman into those of the master and his office assistants. This led also to a division of labour; men of general knowledge were only exceptionally required as foremen or outdoor superintendents: and the artificers became, in process of time, little more than attendants on the machines.'
>
> (Berg 1980: 196)

Foster gives industrial control and its achievement a wider social and political significance: 'the crucial integrating authority system was now authority in industry' (Foster 1977: 223).

Describing developments in the engineering industry in Oldham in the 1860s he says that the industry's new technology demanded a new structure of authority 'in which the skilled top third of the labour force acted as pacemakers and taskmasters over the rest' so that the skilled men became involved in the work of management of a labour force that was deliberately being de-skilled (Foster 1977: 228).

He also argues, rather more equivocally, that these strategies were accompanied by a third, a deliberate attempt by the employers to 're-stabilize' the social situation that they had so severely disturbed in the process of industrialization. The middle classes of Oldham had deliberately and effectively tried to win labour from its working-class vanguard, they had done so by making concessions, albeit on their own terms. Foster adds that it

> 'has to be recognised that something more was involved than just the old-style control from above. In time there does seem to have developed a cultural receptiveness to employer attitudes among certain sections of the labour force, most typically expressed in the development of Wesleyan Methodism.'
>
> (Foster 1977: 236)

That same 'cultural receptiveness' was the aim of a number of developments described by Berg, who argues that the development of the Mechanics Institutes was 'identified with demands for a newly adaptable labour force and with the hardening of social hierarchies within the work process' (Berg 1980: 146). Education, factory development, mechanization, and the development of workers all became bound up in the relationship between moral virtue, science, and economics. The connection between technological improvement and economic development was, she says, developed in the Mechanics Institutes:

> 'It was meant to contribute to the formalisation of hierarchies in the labour movement. The skilled artisan was to be separated from unskilled common labour, and both were to be detached from the middle class. This design for creating a "labour aristocracy" was complemented by efforts to contribute to the discipline of the labour force'.
>
> (Berg 1980: 179)

The three strategies, if that is what they were, can be distinguished as mechanization, labour differentiation, and education. The first prescribes tasks, routines, times, and specification as though by reference to some immutable logic. The second relates the organization that follows from that logic to an order of different jobs with different grades, levels of authority, and pay. The third teaches the principles upon which the first two modes are laid out and goes beyond them to demonstrate their intricate relationship to an economic order that, because of its component of free competition, has immanent associations with political freedom and moral order. The result is something very like the hegemony that, according to Gramsci, begins, in an industrial society, at the factory bench.

It is not our business here to debate the extent of this ruling hegemony in present-day industrial society. We need only note the acquiescence among radical critics of the capitalist production process in the view that coercion is not a sufficient means for the employer to attain his goals. Goodrich, writing in 1920, quotes several examples of the almost absolute power claimed by employers and agreed to by trade unions in a number of collective agreements:

> 'Each employer shall conduct his business in any way he may think advantageous in all details of management. . . .'
> 'That Dressers shall not interfere in any way whatever with the management of workshops. . . .'
> 'The Federated Employers . . . will admit no interference with the management of the business.'
>
> (Goodrich 1920: 57)

The employers' position, says Goodrich, is summed up in the words 'discipline' and 'management' which together are used to describe the issues over which the employers are adamant in refusing any share in control. And yet, says Goodrich, 'the phrase almost disappears under analysis' – he goes on to give accounts of the various ways in which management's absolute claim to control is, in practice, checked by trade union opposition, by legislation, or by the strategic counter-reaction of employees to control as such (Goodrich 1920: 61). Nine years earlier, F. W. Taylor had described the existing state of affairs in employment in all the industrialized countries as a jungle of restrictive practices, ca' canny, hanging-out, or soldiering. To the present day, managers never seem to speak with as much authority as when complaining of the limits of their power in the direction of work. And there is no shortage of academic support in arguing that 'traditional approaches to organization and increased efficiency involving specialization, de-skilling and centralized management control have often failed, resulting in low productivity, lack of flexibility and alienation of people from their work' (Bailey 1983: xiii).

Coercion, aided by mechanization, labour differentiation, and education, have not succeeded in achieving labour co-operation. That statement may, in fact, be a truism; by definition coercion cannot produce co-operation. The act of co-operation is, in some measure, at least, voluntary, willed, offered rather than obtained. There may be philosophical and psychological explanations for the need for the employer to achieve co-operative labour from his subordinates. Two other more immediate and practical explanations always accompany the employer's active search for labour co-operation. The first is the increasing technical complexity of the tasks required to be done, no longer to be adequately performed by the willing or unwilling compliance of unlettered children, women, or men. (Such was the case for the Mechanics Institutes in the nineteenth century: Britain needed intelligent, educated, and responsible employees to keep up with increasingly technical production processes and with foreign competition.) The second is that the liberal, democratic employment times in which we live demand that employers seek the co-operation of the employees because the forced labour of unwilling workers is, we are told, inappropriate to the age. This was one of the principal arguments, if such it can be called, used by the Bullock Committee (1977) in support of its recommendations.

The extent to which consent is substituted for coercion as an expectation planned for by the employer varies, of course, with the nature of the work, the organization, and the worker. But *all* subordinate work requires, to some extent, compliance. As Thompson puts it: 'the objective fact of control ultimately depends on the existence of subjective consent' (Thompson 1983: 152). The search for at least a sufficient degree of control explains the recognition of 'the mixed and contradicting motives behind the growth of welfare and personnel management in the U.S.A.' in order to develop more subtle forms of social control than sheer coercion (Watson 1983: 14). It is now increasingly widely recognized among labour process theorists that the relationship between employer and employee is not simply one of conflict engendered by coercion, because capital requires to employ the full potentiality of human beings. Craig Littler points out the dual nature of the relationship between capital and labour, that while capital is constantly transforming the forces of production it must also stimulate, harness, and motivate labour's creative power. Capitalists are therefore driven to seek a co-operative relationship with labour in a market context that limits the potential for achieving co-operation: 'it is the forms of capitalism which can square this circle which are most likely to survive' (Littler 1983: 32).

Perhaps this selection of authorities from all parts of the theoretical compass is sufficient to establish that the employer cannot and will not rely on coercion to co-ordinate the activities of his employees. The nature of his control is more subtle than that, its character is likely to change in different circumstances, and (as all this talk of contradictions and squared circles suggests) the nature of his authority is always likely to be problematic. We shall take up the remainder of this chapter in exploring the nature of the problem.

First, as to the nature of authority itself. Authority is necessary to social activity and to the conduct of industrial, commercial, and administrative enterprise. Watt tells us that 'without authority . . . no community of human beings as we know them can be imagined' (Watt 1982: 107). He makes an important distinction between two usages of Roman republican government: *auctoritas*, a pronouncement, not a right to rule, advice or 'the kind of counsel that should not properly be shunned', and *potestas*, 'a right to issue commands that ought to be obeyed, as well as council that ought to be respected' (Watt 1982: 15). The significance of this distinction for what we have to say about management is that *auctoritas* seems to reside in the statement or pronouncement, while *potestas* resides in he who issues it.

Watt also tells that authority is often associated with reason:

'in some ways of talking about it, [it] must be marked by the appropriate kind of reason or justification, so that whatever lacks that reason or justification cannot be authoritative' (Watt 1982: 19). It is distinguished from *de facto* authority, which is strictly descriptive, concerned with the fact of compliance, not 'with any right to command or obligation to obey' (Watt 1982: 27). So, we can speak of officials or managers who have lost authority over subordinates, but who retain 'a right to their compliance which, in practice, they cannot get' (Watt 1982: 28). The difference in the case of *de facto* authority concerns the familiar confusion with power. Power concerns those situations in which compliance is achieved by a measure of coercion; authority is concerned with compliance which is, in some measure, unforced, unthreatened, and unpersuaded. To speak of people complying with authority implies the possibility that they may not do so.

Authority is often associated with reason, sometimes with rules. In the same way that Weber distinguishes between charismatic, traditional, or rational-legal authority, Watt tells us that the subject must always have some understanding of the rule or reason for obedience. While there is not always a rule, there is usually some reason for the exercise of authority. This means that authority is limited by a context of some kind. If authority means a right to be obeyed then that right cannot be conceived of except in terms of the limits proper to its exercise. The exercise of authority outside such limits or beyond the appropriate context is the abuse of authority, that is, the use of authority that is rightful but that has been exceeded. The proper limits of authority are frequently conceived to be related to some practice with which it is concerned: 'if the instructions of parents or firemen ought to be obeyed, it is in matters to do with child-rearing or putting out fires' (Watt 1982: 105).

Authority, in order to distinguish it from power, is often thought to be subject to the consent of those over whom it is exercised. This seems to be always true of the cases to which Weber adds the qualification 'legitimate' to authority; it is rightful, exercised by an accepted charismatic leader, it is bound by rules, or it is customary. It is certainly true of voluntary organizations to the authority of whose rules and officers we submit ourselves. It is true also of sailors, says Watt, who 'voluntarily subordinate' themselves for the duration of the voyage, and to soldiers for the period of their military service. But it is not true of children in relation to their parents or pupils in relation to their teachers; in neither case have they voluntarily subordinated themselves and thereby consented to the authority exercised over them. But this is surely a special case, confined to the incompetence, even the impotence of the subordinate, the child. It is not difficult to imagine that the act of voluntary subordination to authority is, in such cases, deferred by the child and anticipated by the parent or teacher. When the exercise of authority is justified by successful child-rearing or teaching it will be retrospectively accepted by the subordinate as having been rightful and necessary. Apart from these special cases of deferred legitimation, perhaps we can say that authority *is* usually subject to the consent of those over whom it is exercised.

Is that true of industrial employees? There are two parts to the answer, the first theoretical, the second empirical. It would be tempting to see an analogy between the situation of the employee and that of Watt's soldier. Even in the time of the most severe military discipline, when infractions were followed by field punishments and floggings, the acceptance of military authority began with a voluntary act, accepting the King's shilling. Similarly, the acceptance of the employer's authority begins with the voluntary acceptance of a contract of employment. There are those who see the contract as fundamental to the exercise of authority. But most observers now see it as an inadequate explanation of authority on several counts. It is, in the first place, a fundamentally unequal contract, as Adam Smith was among the first to point out, because the employers are few and the employees are many and because the contract is necessary to the maintenance of life for the latter but not for the former. Although engagement to a period of military service is submission to a more severe regime, it is also a more unusual one and requires (war-time conscription apart) a more truly voluntary act than is engaged in on seeking employment. And once the contract of employment is entered it is notoriously unspecific; even when soldiers were flogged there was a code of discipline, however severe, absent, for the most part, from industrial employment. The contract neither tells the employee what is required of him or what will happen to him should he fail to deliver this unspecified expectation. The contract fails by reference to those other characteristics by which authority is defined: it is not reasonable, there are insufficient rules, and there is no legitimately demarcated context beyond which authority can be judged to be oppressive. The point is made by those very statements of the extent of employers' authority or of managerial rights extracted from collective agreements by Goodrich (see p. 33 above) as grotesquely illustrating the exaggerated, impractical, and therefore unreal nature of the extent of authority claimed by the employer.

But authority there is and it is defined, not in the contract, but in practice. It grows, to begin with, from its close association with power.

The merging of power into authority is particularly likely to occur in some of these categories. Expert power is likely to reside in both *auctoritas*, 'the kind of counsel that should not properly be shunned', and *potestas*, concerning capacity, or the right to issue commands that ought to be obeyed. The authority exercised by the craftsman over the apprentice, or the craft foreman over the craftsman, is almost indistinguishable from expert power. Referrant power similarly suggests a propriety concerning those subordinated to it, a justice and rightness about its exercise acknowledged by those who submit to it. The relation between positional power and authority is more likely to be by association and custom than by justification. The chairman or the managing director exercise not only power by virtue of their control of resources and their ability to reward or punish; their office is also respected as authoritative in itself. In this sense, some part of their influence stems from customary authority, in Weber's sense of the words. And some part of this customary authority descends to subordinate managers until it runs into the sand on the production shop floor where the customary authority of the chairman may be treated with scant respect while his power is still acknowledged.

But the hierarchy of management is permeated, certainly within its own rules, by a traditional, almost instinctive respect for the authority of its superordinate inhabitants. Indeed, one of the possible explanations of the bewildered reactions among managers to questions concerning the foundation of managerial authority is that it is not a problem they have thought about. It is, as we shall see in chapter 6 'not a question that ever arises'. Authority, among managers, is customary, accepted, unchallenged, and unexamined. Because of this implicit acceptance it is projected, equally uncritically, upon those inhabitants of industrial organizations who possess no authority, the manual employees. It may be this uncritical acceptance and this projection that explains the unreality of unitary managerial attitudes to and expectations of shop floor co-operation. Managers may persist in the belief in an authority over the shop floor because it is an evident reality in terms of their own intramanagerial relationships.

How far is that authority accepted across the boundary between management and labour? In one of the few attempts that have been made to measure the legitimacy of managerial power, Gallie, acknowledging the difficulty of task, set out to measure the approval of workers for an 'unbridled managerial prerogative' as against a decision-making process that afforded workers' representatives a right of consultation and a process that gave the workers the right of veto (Gallie 1978: 121). The research was carried out on a comparative basis in two French and two British oil refineries. Broadly speaking, the majority of British workers accepted the current methods of decision making, only a very small minority completely rejecting it. Almost half the French workers, on the other hand, wanted major changes in the way decisions were taken. British workers believed that decisions about work timing, manning, and salaries were all reached by agreement between management and their representatives; on those issues they were 'satisfied with the basic form of the institutionalized' mechanisms of negotiations that had been established. The majority of them apparently believed, in relation to long-term, strategic decision making, that they had little influence but that 'this was a legitimate sphere of decision making for management to keep under its own wing. The feeling was that it was management's job to manage' (Gallie 1978: 145). The French, on the other hand, were much more radically disposed towards the existing authority system: 'one is above all struck by the essential legitimacy of the final structure of power in Britain and its lack of legitimacy in France' (Gallie 1978: 148).

The problem with empirical evidence in areas such as this is what to make of it. It is confined to the petro-chemical industry and that has been the subject of radical examination by Nichols and Beynon (1977) who found much greater evidence of alienation and dissatisfaction with management than had been assumed to exist in that industry. The differences between the French and the British responses can be explained by a wide variety of factors including the character of French management, the relative weakness of the French trade union movement, and the historical significance of syndicalism in the outlook of French workers. As far as the work of Nichols and Beynon is concerned we must recognize that we are concerned to discuss here not alienation but managerial authority. But it seems reasonable to point out that the broad acceptance of the *status quo* in terms of influence upon decision making and the authority of management among British workers is a characteristic more or less agreed upon by radical writers upon British industrial relations who, on the face of it at least, would have the greatest interest in reporting the opposite conclusion.

It is from the other side, as it were, that we get the contrary view. The Industrial Society tells us that 'getting people's commitment to work is the challenge of the age' (IS 1978: 2) and that 'if Britain as a whole is to continue to create the goods and provide the services that are necessary to maintain our standard of living, then our industry and commerce must become more efficient and more productive' (IS: 1980).

The Confederation of British Industry complained of negative and defensive behaviour among employees, of

'the apparent willingness of employees to strike at the drop of a hat, to ignore established procedures, to adopt a winner-takes-all approach to bargaining. In the extreme, they appear alienated, not only from their company but from their union and their colleagues.'

(CBI 1980: 15)

Sir Peter Parker, then chairman of the British Railways Board, concluded that 'if it is any one thing that has failed us in British enterprise, it is the will to work, the leadership of management, the determination to establish common purpose and unity' (Parker 1983: 16).

If the evidence provided by Gallie can be generalized and if the conclusions of radical observers of industrial relations are reliable then the instances quoted of managerial concern about absence of worker co-operation might seem to be misplaced. But it is possible that British workers, unlike the French perhaps, accept both the authority of their managers and their right to manage, while at the same time withholding a degree of co-operation sufficient to satisfy their managers. It is one thing to say that British workers make no revolutionary claim against the authority of their managers and another to maintain that they will therefore co-operate sufficiently to please them. There are several possible explanations for the gap between the acceptance of authority and a sufficiency of zealous co-operation. They could concern the unrealistic expectations of managers or the limited context in which authority is exercised and held in esteem. In this particular respect, it may be significant that Gallie found that the more detailed arrangements of work were believed by the refinery workers to be negotiated, and properly so, while the long-term strategic decision making was for management alone. This could mean that the 'contested terrain', or the 'frontier of control', was more narrowly defined in the British context than it was in the French. It may be that the conservative and un-radical British respect for managerial authority is quite formal and of no great value to management in the pursuit of its productive objectives.

This is to suggest that the comparative strength of British trade unions and work groups (at least until the recent depression) compensates in some way for their lack of radical zeal. It has been argued by Fox and others that this collective bargaining strength causes that lack of zeal. Pluralism, the very theoretical framework upon which collective bargaining rests, 'simply serves, in a somewhat more sophisticated manner appropriate to a society of complex organizations, rising aspirations, and restiveness against authority, the same kind of integrative function as was served by unitary notions in more respectful epochs' (Fox 1974a: 273). The holders of power concede limited influence to their subordinates, making modest concessions so as to avoid the risk of frustrated explosion of more dangerous demands. The method of this accommodation is collective bargaining. It is through collective bargaining that 'unions organise a mass membership, provide career and status opportunities for leaders and establish a pervasive network of participative activities touching upon almost every public aspect of social and economic life' (Fox 1974a: 291). The unions, relying upon collective bargaining 'socialize their members into accepting what it is sensible for them to expect from their work and life'. The area defined by collective bargaining is accepted as incontestable by the lower ranks 'because they are either socialised to see it as legitimate, inevitable and natural, or required to submit to it as an expression of power which they cannot challenge except at disproportional cost to themselves' (Fox 1974a: 293).

But it seems worth observing that it is the managers, who make the concessions in the interests of the maintenance of social stability and of a politically quiescent labour force, who are vociferous in their complaints about the cost of these modest concessions. The CBI has asserted that poor industrial relations have contributed to Britain's unsatisfactory economic performance and that the continuation of present trends 'will present a formidable barrier to industrial efficiency' (CBI 1980: 29), that employers need to act collectively to defend themselves against union pressure, that there has been 'a fundamental shift in the balance of bargaining power in favour of organised labour' (CBI 1980: 15).

It appears that those who are making the limited concessions for the sake of social stability do not see them as modest. If there is a grand conspiracy to give the workers just enough to keep them in their place then either it is conducted at great cost to the managers in whose interest it is constructed or they are acting their part with great skill in exaggerating that cost beyond its real level. And if it is not a conspiracy then it is one of those fundamental explanations of social relationships that depend for their persuasiveness on functions that are not performed by the agents whose interests they serve.

Might it be more reasonable to accept the complaints of managers, employers, and their representatives at face value and to conclude that management has not succeeded in maintaining sufficient authority in the area in which it is their most immediate objective to achieve it, in the control of subordinate labour? The CBI urges that management must 'secure the primary allegiance of employees to the company', that it must be prepared to manage, to control irresponsible behaviour, that it must attempt to influence the direction of social trends; but it is the clear implication of those evangelical appeals that management has not yet done these things. All this suggests that, as management sees it, managerial authority is woefully weak.

In a detailed examination of managerial prerogatives, Storey distinguishes four supports on which management's right to manage is made to rest (Storey 1983). The first is derived from property ownership and from the claim that owners or their agents must be allowed to control the capital assets that they own. The second is an extension of ownership by way of statute law; the right to manage devolves from the responsibility to shareholders. The third is broader, deriving from the general case for economic efficiency; it is in the interests of all of us that managers shall manage as they see fit. Storey points out that this particular argument rests upon an extension of the benefits claimed to derive from the division of labour in which management is seen as a specialized and expert activity. The fourth justification emerges from a belief in natural leaders; it is interesting in this connection that the CBI concludes that because 'there is no longer automatic respect for the position and status of a manager' the circumstances must be 'created in which leadership by management is acceptable – in other words, management by consent' (CBI 1980: 19). Storey suggests that these various claims to managerial authority have been specifically reinforced by the trade unions, partly as a way of placing responsibility on management's shoulders in order to demarcate for themselves a role of permanent opposition. This was certainly the effect of the TUC's acknowledgement of the function of management in the reversal of its earlier claim for a measure of joint control of industry (TUC 1944).

Storey goes on to make two significant points about managerial rights. They are, he says, open-ended in that they prescribe neither the person to whom duty is owed nor the extent or the specific nature of the duty. And, he says, in so far as they are derived from private ownership they amount to a general right held against a transgressor, not a routine obligation from a specific person to do something (Storey 1983). It is noticeable that there is a defensive, even negative character to this version of authority. Its lack of prescription and precision weakens its utility in the engagement of subordinate co-operation, and the claim to a general right against a transgressor suggests an ideological defence turned in quite a different direction.

It may be that such defences as are available in Britain are defences of ownership rather than management, available against the threat of nationalization or even against proposals for the rational, oligopolistic reorganization of sections of British industry. The BBC television series 'All our Working Lives' has given instances, time and again, of reluctance among British employers to sacrifice their independent control of their companies in favour of a measure of urgently recommended centralized direction in their industries. Decline in the coal-mining, motor manufacturing, and textile industries were all attributable, in some measure, to this spirit of independence, to the feeling that it 'went against the grain of a Lancashire mill-owner' to submit to external control over his family firm. To return briefly to the Wiener thesis with which we began: it might be that the problems of British industrial performance lie in a surfeit rather than a shortage of the entrepreneurial spirit and in too fierce an insistance on the part of the third generation to stick to its last rather than retire to the country or to go back to clogs.

It may be that the usual generality of employer ideology in this respect is of no great utility to managers in the more day-to-day direction of affairs in which they must engage. The acquiescence that Storey correctly attributes to the trade unions in the broad delineation of 'management rights' reinforces the view that they may not be constructed for internal purposes and that union respect for them acknowledges recognition of non-negotiable areas that are not in contention within the collective bargaining relationship even when the Labour Party (as the political wing of the union movement) is pressing for the nationalization of a particular utility, but it leaves the managers with no very firm ground to stand upon. Goodrich's reminder of the quite unreal and impractical claims made in statements of managerial rights found in collective agreements (see p. 33 above) suggests that they are of no great use for internal purposes and that any reference to them for the purpose of maintaining domestic order is rhetorical rather than real.

Theoretically, then, managers are rather left on their own. What of the practical or empirical construction? Management would not be the first English institution to have assembled a formidable artillery without attention to ballistic theory. Two of the four legs on which management rights stand are likely to be relevant and helpful to management in the employment relationship. One of them is the claim to expertise leading to efficiency. The other is the claim to leadership, as amended by the CBI to mean 'management by consent'.

Child (1969) made an important distinction between the technical and legitimatory aspects of management thought. The two are related to the three principal needs of managerial action: the technical, the administrative, and the social. It will hardly be necessary to point out that this classification is not precise, that the needs interact with each other, and that some actions cannot be consistently attributed to one or the other. The technical concerns the specification of methods of production or distribution and is likely to be more clearly the concern of management specialists or lower-level managers with primary responsibility for production or distribution. It is also the area of uncertainty in which professional activities like engineering overlap with the more general responsibilities of management. The administrative aspect is to be understood in the sense that Simon (1976) used the term in *Administrative Behaviour*, concerned with the more asbtract matters of the organization of functions, levels, communication, command, monitoring, and control. The third, the social, is concerned with the enterprise, whatever its economic purpose, as a social system occupied by both individuals and groups, set out both in terms of formal (administrative and technical) requirements and informal social characteristics. To some extent it is possible to see the claim to managerial expertise retreating or evolving from the first to the second to the third: from the technical to the administrative to the social.

Commenting on the development of supervision in the engineering industry, Melling says that

'at this stage of industrialisation, employers could not afford to leave the delicate technical problems to lower deputies unless they were of a high calibre themselves. Such a brilliant assistant as Joseph Clement made an excellent foreman as well as an accomplished technical innovator in the works of Bramah at London. Again, his importance to a successful master was as a co-ordinator of men and materials as well as the designer of fruitful modifications.'

(Melling 1982: 257)

He goes on to point out that the position of foreman in the mid-nineteenth century was a 'fluid composition of responsibilities which enabled the holder to handle skilled tradesmen and, on occasion, to become a manager or a partner or to begin their own concerns' (Melling 1982: 258). Nasmyth, in the auto-biography edited by Samuel Smiles (Smiles 1891), speaks of a network of managerial and supervisory relationships largely combined with technical matters and mutual respect for skill and accomplishment. The production side of the steel industry within our own memory was managed on the basis of jobs strictly demarcated by trade and seniority, providing a hierarchy of experience respected in itself and because it was deemed to accompany status and skill.

There is little doubt that developments in the managerial division of labour have superseded technical proficiency as the basis of management and supervision to the point where functional specialisms develop quite separately from the main 'line' of management. In other industries where technology was not so central to the production process or where commercial operations, financial resourcing, and control were relatively more important, other kinds of managers were always of consequence. While men like the Stevensons were important in the early development of the railway companies the later managers are better exemplified by Mark Huish, described by McKenna as 'one of the foremost managers of the Victorian age' (McKenna 1980: 33). As manager of the London and North Western Railway Company, Huish was responsible for the negotiation of numerous grand commercial alliances and treaties, for devising and introducing a system of financial accounting and control, for a pricing and tariff system, and for influencing the character of employee relationships in the company. Huish had been not an engineer but an officer in the Indian Army.

The contrast between these two modes of management, the technical and the administrative, is the subject of a recent discussion on approaches to management in Britain and West Germany (Child *et al.*: 1983). In Germany, the authors say, the emphasis is on *technik*, the products and methods of manufacture; in Britain it is on the control and monitoring role of 'professional' specialists *not* directly concerned with manufacture. Perhaps we can clear away some of the obfuscations about this argument by suggesting that 'professional' is used in such an uncertain way as to justify quotation marks in the early occasions on which it is used; that its connotation is so catholic as to include 'professional' specialists defined to broadly as to include personnel specialists (who might like to be professionals but are not); and that the discussion sometimes encompasses the professionalization of management *per se*, the claim that management is a 'professional' occupation. Allowing for and leaving aside these uncertainties, what the authors call 'professionalism' has, they say, promoted the importance of staff functions and encouraged a splitting of non-routine elements. (It is not our business here to go into the other arguments of the paper, concerning the character of the two educational systems and comparative patterns of career development.) The paper suggests that the British move away from technical education for *technik* as the core of management was related to Wiener's argument about a 'change of direction' during the middle decades of the nineteenth century. This is to return to all the weaknesses of that catch-all argument; it was, as we have noted, for sticking to engineering, production, or *technik* that both British Leyland and Rolls-Royce were blamed for their difficulties. The point of these criticisms was to suggest, sensibly so it seemed to many, that there was more to the management of a large enterprise than the maintenance of its production process, whether one called the alternative 'professional' or not. The distinction between Brunel or Nasmyth on the one hand and Huish on the other is, roughly speaking, between the technical and the administrative modes of management. We are making the distinction here in order to suggest that legitimation of managerial authority has largely moved from the one to the other as the craft skill basis of production has ceased to be important. The complex and disparate set of skills involved in shipbuilding has given way long since to the effective organization and administration of shipbuilding, indeed, the survival of the craft skills and the closeness of management to them is said to be one of the 'traditional' problems besetting the British shipbuilding industry.

Littler suggests that there were three fundamental patterns of employer or management and labour relationships that emerged from the nineteenth century (Littler 1983: 61). The first was based upon a pattern of family ownership and control, found often in cotton spinning. The second was founded upon production largely controlled by master craftsmen with apprentices bound to them and not to the owners, found typically in iron production and ship construction. The third was concerned with work organized in gangs under a ganger or gang boss. All three systems, says Littler, afforded a degree of legitimated independence to labour and none of them was accompanied by any general theory of management, of organization, or of labour control. It is possible that the 'legitimated independence' that they afforded was incompatible with any theory of management that requires or entails a measure of labour control.

The development of such a theory, or at least of several efforts to construct one, followed, if it was not caused by, the falling profit levels of the 1880s. The workshop reorganizations of the 1890s in the British engineering industry produced 'the first stirrings of systematic management' (Littler 1983: 84). In some industries, however technically advanced they may have been (perhaps even because of their technical development), one gets the impression that attempts to develop systematic management in terms of recruitment, career development, and the formulation of some notion of the function of management had to wait until the 1920s or beyond.

Attempts to develop management theory (the point of which, Child reminds us, is legitimating as much as it is 'technical') take two broad forms: they are administrative or social. Both have to wait for the demise of the craft-based technical control of production. Indeed it is possible that no theory of management has emerged from or accompanied its technical mode of behaviour. As soon as craft, engineering, or *technik* has to be related to cost and quality control, to machine utilization and scheduling, to manpower resourcing and flexibility, technical control has given way to a more broadly based management, the consequence of which is likely to include the displacement of the engineer to a staff position, the de-skilling of the craftsman, and the redundancy of the craft supervisor.

Administrative theory began to develop towards the close of the nineteenth century with the introduction of more complex systems of piece-work and incentive payment and the accompanying and necessary introduction of wages departments capable of administering the complex processes of calculation, timing, and costing that were required. The widely acknowledged formalization of such theory was the introduction in the United States of F. W. Taylor's systems of 'scientific management'. It was preceded in Britain first by the substitution of foremen for the internal labour contractor or the ganger. Littler tells us that the considerable power of the foreman 'started to be modified almost as soon as it had emerged from the decay of internal contract' (Littler 1983: 87). It was eroded by the development of specialist responsibilities (like rate-fixing), by the emergence of central administered payment systems, by the decay of personal wage bargaining, the increasing importance of shop stewards, and the gradual bureaucratization of wage negotiations to which administrators and trade unions contributed. The demise of the foreman's power, symbolized by his dismissal or resignation from the responsibility for hiring and firing is, by now, one of the best-recorded and analysed stories.

Scientific management formally ended the reign of the supervisor with the introduction of 'functional foremen'. Scientific management fulfilled both the functions distinguished by Child: it served to enhance the administrative ('technical' in Child's terminology) ends of optimum performance and efficiency achieved by detailed analysis and planning of operations; it also served to legitimate management and to secure approval for its exercise of authority by demonstrating that it was expert. Scientific management was thus, although primarily aimed at achieving control by the detailed prescription of performance, also aimed at the achievement of commitment. It can therefore be seen as an ambitious and comprehensive attempt to square the contradiction that usually appears between these two necessary objectives. The synthesis is established by way of the allegiance that is demanded to the scientific laws that are revealed in the process of analysis. There can be no argument about what is to be done or the right way to do it. Once scientific management is extended to the selection of job occupants suitable in terms of physique, capacity, and outlook (like Schmidt), neither can there be any argument about interests and, as production increases so considerably, nor is there much room for disagreement about the division of the spoils.

The legitimacy aspect of scientific management emerged in Taylor's famous claim that his system was more than a way of running industry more efficiently; it 'substituted joint obedience to fact and laws for obedience to personal authority. No such democracy has ever existed in industry before' (Taylor 1911: 217). In pursuance of this version of industrial democracy Taylor pointed out that management's relationship to the production worker was, in appearance at least, to be reversed. The manager was to become the worker's servant or assistant, his main function to ensure that the worker had all the assistance of efficient organization, training, and unimpeded material supply. The manager was to become, in a sense, the production worker's labourer.

That was one of the problems. The legitimatory aspect of scientific management was the principal reason for its downfall, if downfall there has been. Most contemporary accounts agree that scientific management 'failed'. Taylor complained that his 'philosophy' had never been completely applied, that technical components had been accepted in isolation from each other and from the whole system. When scientific management came to be introduced in Britain it was criticized by Cadbury and by *The Engineer* for its inhumanity. Littler tells us that British management found the Bedaux system more acceptable because it 'limited the restricting of management implied by classical Taylorism, and enabled the control system to be clipped onto the existing management structure' (Littler 1983: 115). Littler concludes that the introduction of scientific management in Britain was limited and unsuccessful because it lacked consistent ideological reinforcement, because its introduction coincided with economic depression, and because it encouraged the intense and bureaucratic regulation of the employment relationship by the trade unions.

The resolution of the contradiction between co-operation and control requires the paradox that control has to be abandoned in order to be achieved. The task is deemed to have been too difficult for British management to accomplish. In addition to all the criticisms of its pretensions to science and its limited psychological understanding of behaviour, the most disabling criticism is that managers were not prepared to abandon their status or their formal authority in favour of joint submission to a new democracy in which their real authority would be enhanced. So, we are told, scientific management failed.

Yet its real influence continues to be considerable. It still provides the basis for what we have called administrative managerial theory and for what Child describes as the technical aspect of management. The whole foundation of the apparatus of job analysis, the micro division of tasks, production planning and control, and functional organization lies in scientific management. And, in that such expertise continues to provide the assurance that managers know what they are doing and are doing things the rest of us cannot do, scientific management continues to provide a considerable element of the claim that managers exercise legitimate authority. If such appeals are most effective when they do not have to be articulated, scientific management may be the more successful now that its more overtly political claims have been withdrawn. Gowler and Legge explain to us that

'the rhetoric of bureaucratic control conflates management as a moral order with management as a technical-scientific order, whilst submerging the former. They also demonstrate how, through the management of meaning, the rhetoric of bureaucratic control contributes to management as a political activity concerned with the creation, maintenance, and manipulation of power and exchange relations in formal work organization.'

(Gowler and Legge 1983: 198)

If all this is so, the question is not why scientific management failed but why it has been described as failing. The answer may lie not in management's purpose but in its claim. It may not be that management needs to assure itself of control but that it requires, not merely compliance, but compliance open and acknowledged. Functionally, that is in terms of the requirements of its role within economic organization, it would be sufficient for management to exercise control, particularly of the hegemonic, reality-constructing kind attributed to it by Gowler and Legge. But within organizations as social systems this may not suffice: what management may require in this context is fealty.

The managerial need for fealty has been discussed elsewhere (Anthony 1977). It concerns in part an unavoidable projection of its own commitment and normative compliance with the goals of the organization and the subordinate employees who are not so completely enclosed within the organization's values. It concerns also management's role in the maintenance of the social system, a subject to which we will have to return in chapter 7. And within the relationship of management to the social system of the organization, management's need for its authority to be acknowledged means that the political aspect of scientific management, Taylor's unprecedented democracy, is the one thing that management cannot acknowledge, just as it can never abandon control in order to regain it.

In its social context, management set out to find a basis for its authority alternative to the control provided for it by scientific management. Child points out that the old ideas of self-help allied to *laissez-faire* economic theory were quite inadequate and were rejected in the development of programmes of industrial betterment of welfare. Welfare programmes were of two kinds, says Child: they were aimed at improving the employees' standard of living and culture or they were intended to develop labour managerial policies that would enhance efficiency and welfare at the same time. He quotes Edward Cadbury to the effect that 'the supreme principle has been the belief that business efficiency and the welfare of the employees are but different sides of the same problem' (Child 1969: 37). Welfare policies seemed to offer the prospect of the social legitimation of management authority beyond its attribution to private ownership.

McGivering suggests that the employers' reaction to industrial unrest was a mixture of self-interest, sympathetic concern, inherited responsibility, and a wish to stabilize relationships while protecting their own *status quo* (McGivering, Matthews, and Scott: 1960). The responses, he says, included co-partnership, profit sharing, and the welfare movement. The last of these became an institutionalized response leading to the founding of the Welfare Workers Association in 1913 (the forebear of the Institute of Personnel Management, a direct line of ancestry, although the offspring bears little relationship to its progenitor). McGivering says that the pioneers of welfare work saw it as complementary to strong trade unionism and Child points out that those companies that pioneered systematic policies of labour management were more sympathetic to trade unions than were most of their contemporaries (Child 1969: 37). McGivering adds that the trade unions, however, took a more cynical view of managerial intention in the development of welfare programmes and there is no doubt that trade union opposition contributed to the demise of management's faith in welfare. Welfare, along with paternalism, was relegated to the past, deemed to be irrelevant because of its dubious relationship to efficiency and profit, outmoded by the appeal of scientific management, which was itself only partially accepted. As Littler puts it, the submergence of welfare Quakerism by Taylorite forms of work organization occurred in Britain 'without a context of ideological underpinning' (Littler 1983: 180).

The squaring of this particular circle, between the need to care (in order to justify an appeal for fealty) and the need to be scientifically efficient (in order to control), was made possible, however superficially, by developments in the social sciences and the substitution of behavioural analysis for care.

It took nearly twenty years for the implications of the Hawthorn experiments to begin to have practical consequences in Britain. The appeal of human relations was considerable. It offered an edifice of scientifically acquired evidence in support of the most satisfactory conclusion: that, as Child puts it, 'the requisite skills could release the enthusiasm for co-operation with management which work groups possessed as the result of their deep-felt need for belonging' (Child 1969: 116). It also provided a series of explanations for appearances to the contrary, for the apparent absence of this instinct for belonging and co-operation. The whole story of the development of the recruitment of social science in the service of management is familiar, has been told elsewhere, and it would be repetitive to go through it again (Anthony 1977).

It may be permissible, though, to engage in a brief reminder of the purposes of this development. First, it will be efficient, it will give rise to unparalleled co-operation, transcend or even utilize conflict, and possibly displace the necessity and rationale of trade union organization. Second, it will be good, its very efficiency will be brought about by providing possibilities of achieving the satisfaction of deep human needs in work (at no cost). Third, this marvellous consummation of the hitherto incompatible is to be attained by a newly enlightened and expert management in command of the total technical, social, and human environment. This divine programme and prospect of control is taken to the point when management is advised that it actually controls human happiness, fulfilment, even sanity through the control of work.

Behavioural science, so called, is subsequently joined by a distorted version of political theory that informs management that it is the balancer and arbiter of pluralistic coalitions of interests at the centre of which it sits in objective and impartial judgement, deciding what is in the best interests of all like some colonial palm-tree administrator of justice. The summation of this position is a formidable claim to the exercise of legitimate authority in industry based on a new version of 'scientific' management and accompanying the control provided by the original.

Unfortunately, from management's point of view, the claim is exaggerated and the confidence with which it is made is counter-productive. The productive and manipulative claims of behavioural science have been effectively challenged and the pluralist objectivity of management's position is destroyed by the radical critique's exposure of its special interest and by the unavoidable evidence that it is contested in the workplace.

The case is counter-productive because, resting as it does on the belief that nothing needs to be done except wait for the plum of commitment to fall to management's hand (as long as management has developed the necessary skills for growing plum trees), it actually encourages management to ignore and withdraw from any concern with a conscious policy of employee

relationships. Indeed, for management to appeal for cc
to develop any open ideological programme, wou
confess to a lack of confidence in the social–scientific pro
which has replaced it. Under the regime of neo-1
relations, management can do nothing but wait for the
operation that does not come.

3
A moral model

Thus the development of management thought has moved managers from one impasse into another. Perhaps it would be more accurate to say that the absence of management thought has had this result. Managers have acted, sometimes relying on coercive power to achieve a necessary degree of control, sometimes assuming that control would spread like consequential ripples from the administrative or social networks that they constructed. In each case, the deficiency in control has resulted from an absence of legitimation. In each case, of technical, administrative, or social engineering, the degree of subordinate acceptance necessary to provide legitimation has been withheld because it has never been asked for. The fundamental premiss of each of the modes of managerial action that we have identified (technical, administrative, and social) has been that the subordinate's behaviour would be conditioned rather than willed, triggered by management's action rather than volunteered. The fundamental misconception in each of those three approaches is that the legitimation of authority, its acceptance, and the voluntary submission to control is moral in its character, while the strategies of conditioning are amoral, causal, and mechanical. Management has not achieved legitimate authority because it has taken its authority for granted and has not sought its foundation in rights or obligations. It has, in its pursuit of the techniques of close control, in fact, moved further and further away from a moral form of legitimate authority that was once available to it.

Paternalism is a relationship between master and servant that existed long before industrialization. It was central to the medieval form of political government in which a network of obligations and duties spread out from the king through his lords and their vassals to the lowest serf. This system of social relationships continued to characterize the framework of agrarian England into the nineteenth century. It was summed up in the catch phrase 'property has its duties as well as its rights'. The descent from the old Thomist doctrine that property or political power is justified by the obligations undertaken by those who possess it re-emerged in the doctrine expressed by Coleridge in 1816 when he told the owners of large estates: 'the land is not yours, it was vested in your lineage in trust for the nation' (Roberts 1979: 32). The implication, which was later to be clearly stated by Ruskin, was that landowners should be dispossessed if that trust was not properly met.

Trust is a moral concept and Roberts tells us that paternalists think in moral categories, emphasizing that all relationships, including the economic, should be governed by moral considerations. Paternalism is also backward-looking, conservative, authoritarian, and hierarchic. In face of the crisis perceived by the intelligensia to have been presented by the disturbances of the French revolution and rapid British industrialization, there was a deliberate attempt to achieve some measure of social and political continuity. Helps and Carlyle argued that it was realistic 'to include manufacturers within that sovereign sphere of property that they believed could best grapple with England's social problem' (Roberts 1979: 36). Carlyle, in 1850, called the industrialists the 'aristocracy of fact'. Disraeli saw the need to create a traditional bridge between the new industrialists and old feudal stability (Roberts 1979: 177).

Roberts suggests that paternalism, as a pattern of social

relationship met two needs: it provided a practical model for the management of social affairs and it met, at least to some extent, the need to produce a theory of social organization during a period of social disruption (Roberts 1979: 275). Roberts tells us that between 1827 and 1847 at least twenty books expounding paternalist theory were published (some of them backward-looking and nostalgic, some theological, some expressing a radical toryism), quite apart from numerous novels, pamphlets, and articles suffused with paternalist notions. He suggests that this concern with paternalist ideas followed, in part, from the publication of Burke's *Reflection on the Revolution in France* in 1790. Burke argued from that unassailable and unchanging conservative principle that the existing institutions of society have one great advantage over those proposed to replace them: they work. They are effective because their present form reflects the infinite pragmatic adjustments that have been made to them by past generations faced with changing circumstances. Society, he said, was 'so complex, intricate and fragile that it must be held together by bonds of deference, affection and habit. Society was organic and would, if subjected to the universal formulas of abstract reform, dissolve into chaos' (Roberts 1979: 30).

Apart from a measure of intellectual enthusiasm for paternalism, how effective was it as a practical measure of industrial management? A discussion of that question would tax the reader's patience and the writer's competence. The actual nature of Victorian employment policies is a matter of contested historical territory confused because it was occupied by competing contemporary ideological acounts. On the one hand we have the anodyne accounts of Andrew Ure telling us that the children of the mills took pleasure in their light employment. On the other there is Robert Blincoe giving us an autobiographical account of the sadistic regime of vicious employers and their eager chargehands. Historical explanations similarly differ between the classic account of E. P. Thompson (1968), in which the treatment of children in employment is described as one of the blackest crimes in English history, and Chapman, who takes two employers with unsavoury reputations (one of them the employer of the young Robert Blincoe), Davison and Hawksley of Nottingham, and Needham and Frith of Litton.

Chapman concludes that the evidence suggests that Davison and Hawksley were 'benevolent and enlightened employers', and that 'Needham and his workers with him, were the unhappy casualities of rapid technical and commercial change in a highly competitive industry' (Chapman 1967: 208). The explanation given by Chapman of the unpleasant reputation that both these employers attracted, ill-deserved though it was, certainly in the one case, is itself an interesting comment on different aspects of paternalism and we shall return to it.

There is certainly no shortage of testimony of the good intentions of paternalist employers. There is the 'paradigmatic case' of Titus Salt, building the model village of Saltaire, of 850 stone houses (at a cost of £106,552), the church (£16,000), baths and wash-houses (£7,000), 45 almshouses (rent free with an income of 7/6d per week for single people, 10/– for married couples) for employees of 'good moral character' incapacitated for work because of age, disease, or infirmity (Roberts 1979: 178). There is Oldknow's community at Mellor and his determination to create employment for the males whose families he employed in cotton spinning (Unwin, Hulme, and Taylor 1924: 168). There are the lesser-known cases like Gilbertson, 'managing not only a successful company but . . . also deeply involved in the everyday life of Cwmavon, contributing largely to its religious, educational and social development and attempting to improve the quality of life generally for his employees and their families' (Jackson 1985: 11).

The reasons for this concern or interference as it has been variously described are frequently confused. They often stem from a real moral concern founded in the religion of the employer, sharpened in many instances by what he saw as the dissolute and uneducated habits of his employees. They often, as Pollard (1965) pointed out, follow from sheer necessity and the economic and geographical factors that took the centres of large-scale production to virtually uninhabited territory. In these circumstances, the employer, whatever else his motives, had to house his workers. Gilbertson, for instance

'felt there was no alternative but to accept the role of the leader within his isolated enclave at Cwmavon. . . . His company was dependent on the labour of that community, and he willingly accepted the reciprocal obligation to be its developer, its spiritual and moral protector and its ultimate arbiter in all aspects of its social and economic life.'

(Jackson 1985: 14)

But these obligations, moral and practical, would not stop Arthur Gilbertson complaining in a dispute that 'this is the way the men thank me. I am thoroughly disgusted with the Glynbeudy people, and I will get my money out of the works as soon as I can, and you will see the difference when I have gone' (Jackson 1985: 7).

Mr Gilbertson's petulance was occasioned by a tendency on the part of some of his employees to act independently of his authority and to enable themselves to do so by joining a trade union. Unionism, because of its promise of a degree of independence from the employers' control, has often seemed antithetical to paternalism. James Nasmyth expressed his admiration and respect for the 'rapid and skilful operations in lifting and transporting' of the unskilled labourers he employed and explained that he selected those of them with mechanical aptitude to be trained to operate machine tools. Nasmyth faced a lengthy strike because he insisted on 'promoting workmen according to their merits, and advancing them . . . in proportion to their skill, ability, industry and natural intelligence' (Smiles 1891: 209). He complained that the Engineer Mechanics' Trades Union said that men who had not served seven years were not entitled to the trade and that this 'indolent equality' that the union aimed at was a great hindrance to progress. 'I told them that I preferred employing a man who had acquired the requisite mechanical skill in two years rather than another who was so stupid as to require seven years teaching' (Smiles 1891: 218). Nasmyth brought in sixty-four skilled Scotsmen, brushed aside the union's pickets, and 'conquered the Union in their wily attempt to get us under their withering control' (Smiles 1891: 217).

The opposition of the wool-combers' union to Robert Davison's technical innovation is cited by Chapman as one of the reasons for the poor labour relations and riotous indiscipline that dogged this benevolent employer. But there are other more profound explanations which take us back to Burke's conservatism. Reinhardt Bendix sees Burke as taking conservatism in a new direction.

'In keeping with his interest in the conservative function of religion, Burke admonished the poor to be satisfied with their station in life. But unlike the evangelicals he did not remind the "higher classes" of their Christian duty to excel in their manners and their piety. He claimed instead that the rich would enhance the "general good" by pursuing their selfish interests, "whether they will or not".'

(Bendix 1956: 77)

Bendix argues that Burke's belief that the general good followed from the pursuit of selfish interest helped to undermine the 'traditional' theory of dependence 'according to which the rich had the duty to think for the poor and regulate their lot' (Bendix 1956: 195). It may have been paradoxical, as Bendix says, that this great defender of the traditional order should have contributed to its destruction, but this departure was to prove convenient for the new rising class of manufacturers. The advancement of self-interest to become a matter of obligation and duty was one of the key features of the doctrine of *laissez-faire*.

Such an amoral doctrine came to be quite compatible with a paternalistic policy of employment. Part of Chapman's explanation for Davison's disastrous employment relationship is that Davison was a member of the High Pavement Presbyterian Chapel, Nottingham. The chapel was, in the last quarter of the eighteenth century, a centre of progressive radical thought; its minister, the Rev. George Walker, FRS was 'the voice of radicalism in the east Midlands'; its congregation included a number of important manufacturers. Walker was a friend and correspondent of Joseph Priestly and a former pupil of Adam Smith at Glasgow. Chapman says that the dissenting radicals 'were characteristically upper middle class and paternalistic in their attitude to the working classes. However, in their economic thinking, Priestly and his following accepted the political economy of Adam Smith' (Chapman 1967: 196). These two incompatible elements probably explained the 'fundamental inconsistency' that Chapman identifies in the behaviour of the firm Davison and Hawksley.

'On the one hand, they were clearly anxious to be benevolent employers, and to let it be known that they were acting as Christian gentlemen in their business careers. On the other hand, the political careers of Robert and John Davison, the work regimen established by the firm, and the uncompromising attitude taken to the woolcombers all strongly suggest a doctrinaire attachment to the idea of laissez-faire rather than to the moral teaching of Christianity. Very likely, Davison and Hawksley did not see the two sets of principles as being at variance.'

(Chapman 1967: 196)

But if the employers and the philosophers saw no inconsistency in the turn that paternalist employment policies had taken, their employees did. With an uncanny intuition for the significance of motive rather than good works, Davison and Hawksley's exemplary conduct as employers was met by continuous labour unrest and hostility which included disputes, riots, absconding from work, spoiling work, and threats of arson. It was not only the vested interest in job preservation of the union that the firm offended, it was the innate conservatism of the workers that was affronted by the progressive, scientific, radical Jacobinism of these enlightened employers. In the Nottingham riots of 1794 the property of several chapel-going spinning families was attacked by anti-Jacobean mobs. Chapman comments that 'there is no record of attacks on the industrial or private property of those who conformed with the Established Church and orthodox political mood' (Chapman 1967: 195).

In the transfer of paternalism as a social doctrine from a landowning society to an industrial employment policy the essentially moral character of the doctrine became transformed into the amoral nostrum that it was a duty to look after one's self. From Robert Owen's assertion that his sincerity was tested and approved when he kept on his employees throughout a four-month trade depression, and from Samuel Oldknow's claim that his chief concern was the happiness of his employees, a version of paternalism emerges that seems to extract moral concern for the welfare of the employees. Roberts tells us that the Report of the Royal Commission on the Employment of

Women and Children in Mines (1842–43) is 'almost destitute of examples of employers doing anything for the schooling and health and housing of their employees' (Roberts 1979: 183). There is a subtle shift also from paternalistic care as a feeling of moral responsibility to those members of a community who are known to the employer and a more doctrinal allegiance to a principle of philanthropy that must be directed towards the unfortunate at home or abroad. Traditional paternalists, Roberts tells us, scorned the larger work of philanthropy and the 'indiscriminate, promiscuous benevolence' exhibited by utopians and evangelicals. For many of the manufacturers, benevolence was a matter of theoretical principle rather than feeling. Ashworth, for example, believed that 'his benevolence arose not from *noblesse oblige* but from calculated self interest'. The distinction between the two forms of paternalism, traditional and calculative, may serve to question Bendix's conclusion that paternalism was 'in fact quite compatible with calculating methods of labour management' and that a strict enforcement of discipline and a very efficient organization were quite compatible with relations between employer and workers that were partly 'authoritative' and partly 'amiable, moral and sentimental' (Bendix 1956: 49). There is, indeed, no difficulty in reconciling paternalism and the strictest labour control; paternalism is, in its nature, authoritarian rather than authoritative. But paternalism, at least in its traditional form, is not compatible with calculation. Benevolent care and the absence of harshness, as a Yorkshire agriculturist claimed, are characteristic of landowners because the nature of their occupations and of their property 'are strong inducements to live in terms of intimacy and Christian kindness with their tenants and labourers' (Roberts 1979: 175).

The application of traditional agricultural paternalism to the realm of industry and the 'aristocracy of fact' seemed to shift the nature of the doctrine. John Child distinguishes between two kinds of industrial welfare policy. The first is aimed at improving the living standards of employees and their culture, is fairly altruistic and responsible in character, and often emanates from strongly held religious principles. The second is associated with early labour management policies and is directed at increasing efficiency as the result of improving welfare (Child 1969: 36). This is what is termed here 'costed paternalism'.

It seems to offer every advantage to the employer: a moderate reputation for righteousness, complete control (for the authoritarian characteristics of paternalism are retained), and no obligation to continue to pay for improvement in the conditions of employees beyond the point at which the investment yields a reasonable return in increased efficiency. It is perfectly compatible with the employer's need to put his own interest first; also, it gives rise to behaviour that contrasts oddly with those claims to be concerned from which the employer sets out. Gilbertson's admirable readiness to undertake responsibility for the development of the community of Cwmavon does not prevent him from abandoning the Cwmavon works in 1861 in order to purchase the tinplate works at Pontardawe. The historian of Cadbury's tells us that, in 1929, mechanization brought about a reduction of 3,000 in the number of employees, entirely unavoidable, of course: it would be suicide to shrink from the newest manufacturing processes, 'all that can be done is to mitigate the immediate effects' (Williams 1931: 127).

These and many similar instances suggest ways in which paternalism becomes qualified. There are limits of good or caring behaviour beyond which the employer is not expected to go, either by reference to his own moral standards or to those of his peers. While his responsibilities continue to be exercised up to those limits, it begins to be quite proper for him to submit his welfare policies to the test of providing a profitable return on the capital expenditure they entail.

Fox says that industrial welfare policies demonstrated only that the employers' self-interest did not necesarily demand the harsh treatment of employees; good management required that they be treated generously 'up to the point at which this policy was judged to be yielding diminishing returns' (Fox 1974b: 57). Robert Owen was among the first to claim, in attempting to persuade his fellow manufacturers to follow his example, that they need not be worried because what was good was also profitable. This version of paternalist doctrine itself becomes weakened when the employer's motivation for the provision of welfare to employees is determined not by the meeting of their needs, which will also be profitable, but by the establishment of arrangements (needed or not) that will create dependence that will be profitable. The three paradigms of this shift could be represented thus:

type	behaviour	motive	reward
traditional paternalism	authoritarian and protective	moral	loyal service, approval, and control
costed paternalism	protective, but limited by financial con- siderations	moral and self- interested	approval, control, and profit
welfare management	manipulative	self-interested	profit

Welfare management begins to appear to be more sophisticated than its forerunners in several respects. It is no longer concerned to control labour by autocratic methods or personal leadership because this becomes impractical. When successful paternalist employers grow they develop complex methods of administration and management. One commentator sees Rowntree's appointment of a woman welfare officer in 1891 as 'the first step towards the bureaucratisation of benevolent paternalism' (Bruce 1983). The old autocratic methods of labour control will no longer serve; Arthur Gilbertson was often described by union critics as a kind of antideluvian survival from an earlier age. Welfare management often, but not always, comes to terms with union membership for its employees, with joint consultation, participation, and even collective bargaining. Child says that, by the end of the nineteenth century, in firms like Lever's, Renold's Chain, and Mather and Platt, industrial welfare programmes had merged with significant labour management policies, with selection and training schemes and high wages. He adds that the companies that provided regular systems of labour management were more favourable to trade unions than were most others. The pioneers of welfare management often saw it as complementary to strong trade unionism but differed from trade unionists in their belief that employers could achieve social justice by being good. The American approach to welfare was often described as less philanthropic than the British.

We are not discussing clearly discernible categories of managerial behaviour, of course. Human motives are often mixed, always so in the management of work. But there do seem to be differences in the balance of motives mixed into traditional attitudes of employers and those of modern managers. We must also guard against the dangers of a nostalgic attitude to the past, particularly as commentators like Bendix tell us that paternalism is often 'an image of society which appeals to our sympathies because it contrasts personal attachments and bought services' (Bendix 1956: 31). With these reservations in mind, what is the essential significance of the paternalist model for modern employment relationships? The question may be addressed (it is doubtful if it can be answered) by contrasting its claims with its limitations.

The advantages of adapting the new conditions of mass manufacturing to the traditional relationships and obligations of an established society were apparent not only during the period of rapid industrialization – they are as apparent today. Paternalism is a model of social relationships that could be seen to meet the anxieties that have preoccupied social theorists since the industrial revolution. The model, while offering peace and cohesion, also incorporates a distinctly un-egalitarian, un-democratic view of the role of subordinates: they are to do what they are told while their protection and development is left in the hands of those who are more powerful and more educated than themselves. This is a nostrum out of tune with the times but it finds perverse echoes from strange places. It is none too different from doctrines of the dictatorship of the proletariat and the supremacy of the Communist Party in economic planning, in the direction of education, and in the embodiment of the good of the community. Paternalism is also fairly realistic by reference to the radical analysis of employment relationships that concludes that the employers and their managerial agents possess great power and almost infinite means of preserving it. If so, then, short of the replacement of the employer, it may be better that he should exercise his power under the constraint of moral responsibility.

The principle characteristic of paternalism, at least of the model if not the practice, is its moral quality. It is based entirely upon the reciprocity of care and obligation; the one justifies and demands the other. The relationship of reciprocity is destroyed as soon as the moral characteristic is withdrawn. It is important to recognize that this is not a social pattern that was unveiled by tory squires or that emerged only from feudal society. Some anthropologists argue that it is an inherent characteristic of all small and stable communities (Redfield 1960). Alvin Gouldner, arguing from anthropological evidence, concludes that there is a 'norm of reciprocity', a recognition of interlocking rights and duties that provides a 'mutually gratifying pattern of exchanging goods and services' creating a relationship of mutual dependence. It is a characteristic of the norm of reciprocity that its rights and obligations are not subject to precise calculation, they are vague and indeterminate, characteristics that themselves contribute to stability because there is always a certain degree of 'ambiguity as to whether indebtedness· has been repaid' (Gouldner 1960: 161–79). An attempt to calculate precisely the degree of reciprocal obligation or the value to be returned for help or kindness would, in fact, entirely destroy the purpose and the effect of the service given. As Fox puts it: 'the greater the degree of conscious calculation which underlay it the more likely was such manipulative intent to show through and promote cynicism among the very people from whom it was designed to evoke trust' (Fox 1974b: 58). The network of obligation is general rather than specific, the attempt to offer help for an expected and measured degree of incurred obligation would be counter-productive. I am obligated to you for what you have done for me, but not if you have done it with the intention of extracting from me a measured response of obligation. The paradox is, as John Ruskin puts it:

> 'treat the servant kindly, with the idea of turning his gratitude to account, and you will get, as you deserve, no gratitude nor any value for your kindness; but treat him kindly, without any economic purpose, and all economical purposes will be answered.'
>
> (Ruskin 1905: 31)

The limitations of this pattern of relationship in its application to the management of economic enterprises do not concern the limited capacities of the employers so much as the pressures that were imposed upon them. The whole calculative and bureaucratic network seems incompatible with a relationship of generalized trust. That may be the fundamental explanation of the degradation that we have described as taking place from the traditional model of paternalism, through costed paternalism to welfare management, so that, ultimately, the employer provides a precisely measured amount of welfare in the expectation that it will bring him a profitable return in greater labour co-operation, reduced absenteeism, or fewer strikes. And at that point, as Ruskin warns, welfare loses its point because the employees see that it is a cynical device that imposes no kind of obligation upon them. Thereafter, welfare policies begin to fall out of fashion because they 'do not work'.

The pressures that contribute to this process of decay and decline come from the market and the overriding requirement of efficiency and profitability. McGivering says that the obligations of the employer towards employees are replaced by obligations to the business, the company, the shareholders, which have to be met before any other duties are discharged. In these terms, Bruce points out a fundamental incongruity between the doctrines of paternalists and the actual state of labour relations in their factories. The explanation, he says, 'is not in the loss of a specific philosophy of industrial relations on the part of Quaker employers, but rather in the exigencies thrown up by the capitalist mode of production' (Bruce 1983: 7). Storey says that there is a structural division of interest between those who buy and those who sell labour power that produces conflict irrespective of programmes of good communication, effective leadership, or good human relations, and that 'rational' activity is determined by reference to the arbitrament of the price mechanism and the pursuit of profit (Storey 1981: 24).

Moore tells us after surveying the paternalist policies of the coal-owners of the Deerness valley in the Durham coalfield:

'It was possible to put these attitudes into practice in a period of relative prosperity, or when there were prospects of trade improvement. Compromise and arbitration, the processes of bargaining, could operate in this situation. The reciprocity implicit in such procedures could be reinforced by patronage in the villages. But when trade declined severely and continuously with no prospect of improvement, the burden of maintaining the relationship became unbearable to the men. They reacted with collective political power; this not only breached the reciprocal relationship but spelt economic disaster to the owners . . . who in turn responded politically, and with greater force. Punitive measures after the owner's victory were almost inevitable, and as J. W. Pearce had predicted, a complete victory for the masters was a disaster. The management offered no semblance of paternalism in their relations with the villagers after the events of 1926.'

(Moore 1974: 92)

The question, then, is whether, armed with the instruments of realistic social analysis that enable us to see power relationships as they are and not as they are presented to us, we see paternalism as outmoded by its essentially inegalitarian view of labour and by the limitations imposed upon its moral ambitions by the market in which it must operate?

It is important to recognize first the distinctions we have made between paternalism as an essentially moral pattern of employment relationships and the decomposed versions that make it a barely distinguishable pattern of bureaucratic, rational management. It is not only the environment in which paternalism operates that changes – paternalists also change. We have seen the doctrine move from a robust old tory belief that the obligation to obey those in authority is reflected in their duty to care, to a liberal enlightened belief in progressive technique and progressive labour policies, and, finally, to sophisticated programmes of labour and personnel management. It is not only the market context that makes paternalism outmoded, apparently paternalism itself has resigned.

To assert that paternalism continues to provide a possible model of employment relationships would therefore seem to be foolhardy. The assertion faces formidable obstacles, not least from the market that severely constrains any employer's capacity, granted his intentions, to care. The obstacles include, as we have seen, developments in employer ideology, like self-help, *laissez-faire*, and managerial bureaucracy, which are virtually incompatible with the old model so that the paternalism of the owner comes to be replaced by the 'professionalization' of management. The later (or decomposed) versions of paternalism are related to a belief in progress and improvement and are incompatible with a view that sees labour as permanently subordinate, dependent, and weak. Thus, welfare management begins a process of development that Marx completes in the final independence of the proletariat from any control at all. Any version of paternalism that sees it as concerned to educate and develop independent labour must see it as also contributing to its own demise; the paternalist employer, like the familial relationship on which the metaphor is based, disappears from the scene when the children mature, achieve independence, and leave home. So theorists of employment relations (and there is a rare convergence of radical and orthodox in this respect) conclude that paternalism is a transitional phenomenon in the development of industrialization.

Yet it survives. A list of a dozen or so of the most successful companies in Britain would include names like Marks and Spencer, Cadbury-Schweppes, Unilever, ICI, W.D. & H.O. Wills, British Petroleum, in the employment policies of which some elements of paternalism can still be identified. And these are companies in which paternalism has overcome the almost insuperable disadvantages of great size, the dominance of bureaucratic managerial systems of control, and the depersonalization of ownership. In how many other, small companies is the paternal direction of the owners continuing to be exercised comparatively unchecked? If paternalism is a continuing phenomenon, is it out-moded like some archaic survival of a pre-industrial age?

There are some considerations that suggest that it is not, that it may continue to provide a realistic pattern of employment relationship. The first is that it must be a pattern of an employment relationship. This is not quite the truism that it sounds. It is not necessarily a criticism of paternalist employment policy to say that when it is subjected to severe economic strain it is likely to cease to be paternalist shortly before it ceases to provide any employment at all. The souring of relationships and the harder policies of the coal-owners of the

Deerness valley that were described by Moore coincided with the permanent decline in the viability of the Durham coalfield. Paternalism cannot survive, at least in the economy that we have created, unemployment and we may expect care and reciprocal obligation to be diminished before the employment of which it is a feature is itself brought to an end.

By extension, it is not in itself a denial of either the practical or the moral advantages of paternalism to say that it is a mere gloss upon the employment relationship which is itself economic in its foundation. In its extreme form this criticism suggests that that economic foundation, in capitalist society, is exploitative and that paternalism is merely a device to enable exploitation to go on unnoticed and unchallenged. Of course if one anticipates the end of capitalism with impatient pleasure then anything that supports and prolongs it will be condemned, but that view in itself does not suggest that capitalist employment is quite incompatible with the exercise of moral care. Indeed the objection is that such policies are likely to be successful, not that they are impossible. In the 1892 strike, says Moore, the dispute was conducted 'in a quiet and orderly fashion' in the Deerness valley while troop movements were taking place elsewhere in the coalfield, the difference no doubt explained in part by the contributions made by the Deerness owners to relief funds for strikers (Moore 1974: 87–8). In an odd way the compatibility of a relationship of economic exploitation and of co-operation has latterly come to be recognized by Marxist critics of capitalism. In recent discussions of the labour process we are reminded that the relationship between capital and labour is filled-in and maintained by necessary procedures of co-operation and collaboration, that the measure of the successful capitalist employer is the extent to which he can resolve the contradiction in his relationship with his employees, that explanations of capitalism purely in terms of exploitation are no longer adequate. Further restatements of old doctrine, now characterized as 'crude determinism', tell us that economic forms of relationships between men do not determine their conduct and outlook, that their relationships can be modified because men are moral agents and not economically conditioned puppets. Capitalists, too, can presumably modify the relationships in which they find themselves.

The more moderate criticism, that paternalist care is hypocritical or unreal because it is accompanied by economic self-interest which it serves, is more easily answered. If men and women were to concern themselves with each other's welfare only from pure and unmixed motives of selfless love, then few social relationships could be expected to survive such Jesuitical rigour. Workers are brought together out of necessity but their culture and their traditions are formed out of affection and trust undemeaned by their economic foundations. The economic base on which their relationships with employers and managers rests similarly does not discount the reality of loyalty on the one hand and care on the other. No one but a zealot, of one kind or another, would prefer an employer who behaved with unmitigated economic selfishness to one who demonstrated some affection and responsibility, even were the demonstration less than sincere.

The charge of condescension is a more important one because it implies both inequality and its acknowledgement in relationships between employers and workers. The change in the meaning of the term 'condescension' is interesting. In pre-democratic times the difference between the status, privilege, and power of the lord in his castle and the poor man at his gate was apparent to all, so that if the lord stooped to help the peasant his condescension was a matter to be acknowledged. Once those differences began to be questioned and regretted, condescension began to be seen as arrogant in one party to the relationship and humiliating to the other. So, paternalist care on the part of the employer is seen to imply inferiority in the situation of his employees. But the inferiority of the one and the superiority of the other is denied, at least in terms of their respective rights. Differences between the two in terms of access to educational opportunity, cultural provision, political influence, health care, are not justified but explained by the vastly greater power enjoyed by the employer and the comparative weakness of the employee. In order to adjust these differences in some degree, the power of the employer is to be curtailed and of the employee to be enhanced by a variety of reformative or egalitarian measures. But every explanation of the situation agrees that these amendments and adjustments are necessary because the employer *is* in a dominant position in relation to the employee. Whether the employer owns the means of production or whether they are controlled by managers who do not own them, the relative weakness of the worker remains considerable. The objection to paternalism is that it acknowledges this difference. If the employer is required or even allowed to exercise care and responsibility towards employees who are dependent upon him then his domination over them is given *de facto* recognition. And the power of the employer cannot be acknowledged openly because of disapproval of its consequences and a wish to diminish it. The condescension of the paternalist employer cannot be tolerated because of the fear of legitimizing his power by conferring *de jure* recognition upon it. The objection to paternalist employers is in part an objection to employers *per se*.

It is also an objection to their power. Fox is right to say that, although there are many worse patterns of relationship, paternalism 'is open to the criticism which can be made of all relationships which rest on a highly unequal dependence of one party upon another. They are potentially demeaning to the weaker participant' (Fox 1974b: 50). It may be, as he goes on to say, 'a central principal of Western liberal culture that social institutions should provide free and equal scope for the expression and development of the human spirit' (Fox 1974b: 51), but that may also be a central weakness in the liberal tradition. There is no evidence that any form of the employment relationship can eradicate the fundamental inequality in power that it is bound to express. Its inequality can be modified by, for example, collective bargaining but Fox tells us elsewhere that such modification is strictly limited in its extent (Fox 1974a). It cannot be a fundamental criticism of paternalism to say that it reflects the inequality of employment relationships if that inequality is ineradicable. It is certainly a real criticism of a particular form of the employment relationship to say that it fails to limit or qualify the inequality of power between employer and employee, or that it exaggerates it to the point of demeaning the employee's position, subordinate though he is. But traditional paternalism, based as it is upon the exercise of moral care and concern for the well-being of the subordinate, cannot demean his position.

Decayed or later versions may do so and, ultimately, these

forms run out in a totally one-sided relationship in which the employer tries to have it both ways by abandoning care and requiring trust: the

> 'employer chose less and less to rely on the employee's spirit of give and take, but sought the output or work performance he wanted by imposing more tightly defined, low discretion job programmed work sequences, closer supervision and harsher discipline. Yet while asserting a low-trust pattern over the employee, he hoped for a high-trust response in the form of willing compliance, loyalty and a ready confidence in his leadership.'
>
> (Fox 1974b: 55)

But trust, Fox adds, was not forthcoming: 'men respond to low trust with low trust' (Fox 1974b: 55).

There is no doubt, however, that some versions of paternalism can become oppressive. Littler says that one of the essential characteristics of paternalism is an employer concern with the life of the employee outside work and he cites as an example the social supervision exercised by Henry Ford over his workers before they could qualify for the payment of $5 a day. Against such intolerable surveillance it is perfectly reasonable to distinguish between proper and improper areas of influence over workers' lives and to insist that the moral character, family life, and personal behaviour of employees should be no business of their employers. At least, it would *seem* to be perfectly proper, but some qualifications may have to be accepted. There might be one concerning the necessary exercise of 'extra-mural' responsibility in periods of rapid industrialization, such as England in the eighteenth century. Even the case of Ford might have something to be said for it in terms of his employment of immigrant labour and the need to promote their adaptation to 'the American melting-pot'. The undue and extended influence of employers beyond the work-place can, ultimately, present a threat to democracy. Such objections are real but they are directed at the abuse of a relationship rather than the relationship itself. It is because the strength of authority in industry is so great that the potential influence of those who exercise it is so enormous. The reality of that strength and the very real difficulty of controlling it by programmes of nationalization or of syndicalist control are the reasons for suggesting that it should be exercised, literally, with care and that it should not be abused either by insufficient attention to the needs of employees on the one hand or by manipulating those needs in the interests of authority on the other.

The first justification for an element of paternalist care in the relationship of employment is that it is, or it becomes, a contradictory relationship. This is more usually seen as a weakness than as a strength, one of the many contradictions in capitalism that will contribute to its demise. But organizational theorists are increasingly pointing to the complexity and the contrariness of organizations. They cannot be seen as bureaucratic structures rationally directed at the achievement of goals. Nor can they be seen as profit-making associations driven by the pursuit of economic goals. They are these things, but they are other things as well. Watson reminds us that organizations are people but that people also use organizations: 'In effect, organizations serve many more purposes than simply producing the goods and services which, at first sight, give them their purposiveness' (Watson 1983: 22).

Littler points to the specific contradiction involved in the relationship between capital and labour: while capital must constantly transform the resources of production it must also seek a co-operative relationship with labour; while labour resists subordination it has an interest in maintaining co-operation with capital. The employer must stimulate labour attitudes that are consistent with the maintenance of future profits, but policies designed to produce such attitudes are constrained by the need to make profits in the context of the market. The successful forms of capitalism are those, says Littler, that can square this circle (Littler 1983: 32–3).

There is some evidence to suggest that paternalism provides us with one of those successful forms. Some of the most prosperous contemporary firms maintain strongly paternalistic elements in their employment policies. There is even a suggeston that, in the most downright oppressive and exploitative relationship that can be imagined to exist between owner and labour, paternalism makes the relationship 'work'.

Eugene Genovese begins and ends his study of slavery in the

southern United States with a discussion of the significance and function of paternalism in the institution of slavery. For the slave-holders, he says

> 'paternalism represented an attempt to overcome the fundamental contradiction in slavery: the impossibility of the slaves ever becoming the things they were supposed to be. Paternalism defined this involuntary labor of the slaves as a legitimate return to their masters for protection and direction. But the masters' need to see their slaves as acquiescent human beings constituted a moral victory for the slaves themselves. Paternalism's insistence upon mutual obligations – duties, responsibilities, and ultimately even rights – implicitly recognized the slaves' humanity.'
>
> (Genovese 1975: 5).

It also served to identify the slaves with their community rather than with their class. In this sense, paternalism reduced the possibility of class consciousness and class antagonism to slave-holding. But it also served, paradoxically, to undermine the relationship of naked economic exploitation that slavery is intended to create. In this way, 'the slaves, by accepting a paternalistic ethos and legitimizing class rule, developed their most powerful defence against the dehumanization implicit in slavery'. Southern paternalism, says Genovese, mediated between irreconcilable class and racial conflicts: 'it was an anomaly, even at the moment of its greatest apparent strength' (Genovese 1975: 7).

It was an anomaly also because the institution of slavery that it supported by such mediation was ideologically unacceptable and economically outmoded. Its own 'undermining' of the institution of slavery may have done more to sustain than to destroy it. It is, in any case, unnecessary to point out that we are not engaged in an examination of the relevance of slavery as an employment relationship. The point being laboured is that even if we take the worst, most brutal, most exploitative model of relationship, paternalism can be seen to soften its hardness, to require a recognition of the humanity of the partners in what is otherwise a plainly economic relationship. If paternalism illuminates and reveals the contradictions of slavery, to the proper confusion of the parties to it, then it may be equally valuable in revealing the contradictions of less extreme forms of relationships between owners and workers. This is why the frequent criticisms of paternalism's contradictions, of the impossibility of imposing a moral veneer on the realities of an economic relationship, miss the point. The very inconsistency of paternalism, the harsh realities that expose the limitations of the extent of its care, reflect the confusion and contradictions in the employment relationship itself. Not only does paternalism reflect reality – by accepting moral responsibility as a part of that reality it mediates between humanity and economic exploitation. The search for a more consistent and less contra-dictory model of relationship will have one of two likely effects: it will drive out humanity from the employment relationship (the tendency of 'monetarism') or it will drive out economic realism (the tendency of socialism). Between the awfulness of one alternative and the ineffectiveness of the other, paternalism is a model that is worth re-examination.

4
The retreat from responsibility

In whatever version, and whatever the flaws of that version, paternalism was a model of relationships in which the employer accepted, even insisted upon, the exercise of responsibility for his employees. Authority was concomitant with care, both were exercised by the employer who was the only source of policy and direction. This relationship broke down. The general view, that it is now archaic, that it was out of tune with the times so that progress explains its disappearance, has two weaknesses. It is inaccurate and it prevents a more complete understanding of the abandonment of paternalism by many, but not by all, employers.

We have already engaged in a brief examination of one reason for its decline. It did not end suddenly: it changed, so that subsequent versions of paternalism more clearly revealed contradictions that, once observed, demanded further adjustments which weakened the model. It was impossible to reconcile it with ideologies of *laissez-faire* and self-help which, although their influence may have been exaggerated, persuaded some employers that the constant exercise of care was not only expensive but unnecessary and even wrong. Such self-interested conclusions might have become particularly acceptable in the metal manufacturing industries, which had been particularly sympathetic to paternalism, after the erection of McKinley tariffs in North America. The growth of trade unionism was also, if not inimical, unpropitious. The old unions of independent artisans, while sharing an almost neighbourly view as to the employer's authority, also shared his view of the importance of independence and autonomy; attitudes proper to men whose knowledge of the trade could and sometimes did set them up as masters in it. The new unions, for whom association was a necessary defence against employers distant from themselves in every respect, were singularly open to the appeal of socialist theory, which could not accept paternalist employers because it could not accept employers at all. Those trade unions that had been formed by men whose skills, responsibilities, and communities had nourished an employer-like independence, but who were at work in industries in which the facts of capital formation provided an insuperable barrier to entry into mastership (coal-mining and railways, for example), were likely to be influenced by syndicalist theories which stressed the independence of the worker from the employer and the worker's ability to control his trade.

Jackson draws attention to a change in attitudes that was reflected in a change in the law. Gilbertson, on receiving a letter from workmen whom he had dismissed which addressed him as 'our employer', protested that 'I am accustomed to be addressed as "master" (not employer) in my Works' (Jackson 1985: 32). Jackson says that the distinction was significant: 'employer' connoted merely a provider of employment, 'master' connoted power and control. The distinction was, by then, obsolete in law. The terms 'master' and 'servant' had last appeared in a statute of 1867, repealed by the Conspiracy and Protection of Property Act, 1875, which had substituted the terms 'employer' and 'workman', the two becoming equal parties to a civil contract. Both Gilbertson and his men, says Jackson, would have been aware of the change and its significance, of 'the new conception of legal equality between contractual parties, but his words suggest that he was not prepared to accept the egalitarian spirit of the act nor the social philosophy which had produced the "fundamental revolution in the law".'

(Jackson 1985: 33)

That fundamental change and the social philosophy to which it was related stemmed from liberal utilitarianism and its necessary insistence that, if feelings and opinions are to be weighed and counted, one man's are as good as another's. The liberal dilemma to which it leads is the difficulty in maintaining reforming attitudes that are deemed to be good for people who do not approve of them. The employer who acts benevolently so as to develop the knowledge, education, and responsibility of his employees finally becomes responsible to them rather than for them. The manager, if he is not replaced by a workers' council, soon begins to be told that he must manage with the consent of his employees or that he must 'regain control by sharing it'.

Structural changes in industry and the growth in the size of industrial enterprises, if not sufficient in themselves, are accompanied by other changes that are unsympathetic to paternalist employers. The development of specialist agencies of control in production and financial management, depersonalize and obscure relationships between managers and supervisors and employees. The emergence and growth of personnel management as a specialist function, although initially concerned to develop welfare management, ends with a preoccupation with techniques of controlling human resources and with something like a contempt for welfare. Welfare management comes to be despised because, after its substitution for paternalist care for reasons of calculated self-interest, evidence that welfare expenditure does not necessarily produce returns from more motivated workers leaves it with no case in its favour; having replaced moral concern with self-interest there remains nothing to be said for it if it does not pay.

Whatever its weaknesses, paternalism may have been the last coherent outlook that was evolved and expressed by employers in Britain that sought to express a view of the nature of the employment relationship and of expectations of duty and obedience to authority. Statements based upon capitalist private enterprise, even in contemporary Britain, are rare and tentative, perhaps as the result of a sensitive wish to avoid appealing to the increasingly large number of unemployed for co-operation in the pursuit of private profit. The relative silence of the employers is explained by their abdication from the exercise of direct responsibility for engaging the co-operation of labour. The abdication of the employer begins with the emergence of agents, as contractors, and then managers to engage in the direct recruitment and control of labour. These matters become the 'special function', as Marx said, of those representatives of the employer who is then free to enjoy the returns to his capital without the necessity of working. The managers who increasingly become responsible for the control and direction of labour have relationships with employees that are different from and more direct than those of the employers. But they rely upon an authority that, if it is questioned, is made to rest upon the logic of bureaucratic rules and the expertise that they claim for themselves; whatever it rests upon, it is not benevolence or moral concern. Managers, in a real sense, cannot afford benevolence because it requires an overriding personal authority that can sweep aside the appeals of consistency and the constraints of rules. Managers make the rules, and as long as they need them they have to pay them a measure of respect. In this way, the professionalism of the manager replaces the paternalism of the owner. If the manager is to imitate the owner's paternalistic care he must do so within a context that protects his own bureaucratic rather than autocratic position. In this way employer paternalism is turned into welfare management.

But it is dangerous to generalize about the manager in order to distinguish his relationship to the employees from the owner's. Managers come in different shapes, more significantly, in different sizes. The more senior managers, salaried though they are, may be almost indistinguishable from owners, equally autocratic and equally caring. Sir Michael Edwardes describes how unit after unit recommended continued centralization for Leyland Cars, a course backed by a report of independent consultants and a 12 to 1 majority of members of the Senior Car Organization Group. Sir Michael took a different view: 'for the only time in my business career I imposed a decision on senior colleagues against an overwhelming majority view'; he imposed a process of decentralization (Edwardes 1984: 58). It may have been the only time, as he modestly says, but the reader gets the impression that on many other occasions most of his senior colleagues agreed with Sir Michael.

We must constantly remember that managers are differentiated by the level in the organization at which they operate, and by function. Examination of the industrial relations function, in particular, has revealed the importance of intra-organizational bargaining, the negotiation that takes place between different positions within the organization as distinct from the bargaining that takes place across its boundaries. In a fascinating account entitled 'The Ghost at the Bargaining Table', Winkler has described the distance that separates directors from the organization's negotiators and the techniques used by each to control the other (Winkler 1974). Sir Michael Edwardes, once again, demonstrates his understanding of such matters in his account of his refusal to move into the large corporate headquarters of Leyland House, and his preference for an office 'over the shop', the BL salesrooms at 41 Piccadilly. His preference was dictated by his wish not so much to

'dish out authority, as [to] have it "pulled" from you naturally by people in charge of their own operations where products are developed and made and sold. This doesn't happen easily if there are layers of intermediary staffs, at divisional and headquarters level.'

(Edwardes 1984: 18)

The existence of layers of intermediary staff increases the distance between central managers and peripheral executives. It also increases the occasion for internal negotiation between different perspectives and different managerial interests. Such occasions multiply still further when functional specialisms are added to hierarchical levels of management. These are the typical features of large-scale managerial organizations and few of them have the good fortune to be headed by men with the perceptions and energy of a Sir Michael Edwardes who can overcome those tendencies and the concerted efforts of the organization's inhabitants to encourage them. The reader almost infers from an account like *Back from the Brink* that the chief executive is describing a personal crusade conducted against the interests of management in the defence of corporate good. Indeed, in his rigorous pursuit of decentralization, Sir Michael Edwardes seems almost to be acting against his own interest as well as against the express wish of subordinates and colleagues.

Most managers are not so apparently selfless in pushing down authority to those subordinated to them, or so selflessly concerned with the good of the corporation, or so restlessly energetic in combatting the natural tendency of managers to look after their own comfort and status. It is the unusualness of Sir Michael's account that makes it worth telling and certainly makes it worth listening to. The urgent pursuit of control of the corporation's affairs (albeit that the instrument for the attainment of its objectives is defined as 'delegation') and, more particularly, the assumption of responsibility for industrial relations is, in fact, contrary to the path chosen by the controllers of British managerial concerns. That path has, for the most part, been directed at a policy of insulation in which first the owners and then the managers of British industry have protected themselves from contact with, and therefore from the need to develop any responsibility for, labour.

In some respects this seems likely to be an unconvincing account. It is the opposite of most of the explanations for the development of employment relationship policies which reach down from Marx and in which the employer consistently pursues a strategy of closer and more detailed control. That tradition of explanation has recently been qualified by the acceptance of the contradictions in the position of labour control and, particularly, in the need for management to treat labour as a commodity and as part of a continuing social relationship between employer and labour. It remains the case, however, that in any extant explanation of the employer's relationship with labour, control remains the principle function of the former. In Marxist accounts the control is overriding, inevitably directed at the extraction of the maximum surplus value. In Weberian theories of rational bureaucracy, control and its derivative strategies are the fundamental logical imperative, driven by an inherent rationality so powerful as to overcome any vestiges of traditionalistic patterns of work and behaviour.

In more recent pluralistic theories of management, control aimed at the goods of productive efficiency is either one of several contending objectives derived (by some unaccounted but reassuringly democratic osmosis) from the various interest groups making up the community, or it remains paramount, pursued the more effectively as it takes the measure of and allows for the other contending factions and interests. In the first of those pluralist explanations, management (the owner has by now gone or, at least, we do not like to speak of him) is one of many groups although *primus inter pares*. In the second, management's primacy is dependent upon its recognition and adjudication of the squabbles between the rest.

The argument to be pressed here is that this single-minded concern with control, always rationally directed at the achievement of economic goals (exploitation or profit), is quite contrary to some of the historical evidence as to employer strategy and to the contemporary evidence about management.

Allowing for the usual encrustation of nostalgia in any account of a past too distant to be remembered, the pre-industrial employment relationships, we are told, were familial or based on the model of an extended family.

'Up to the eighteenth century . . . work was carried out by *households* and was a combination of self-provisioning subsistence, wage labour and by-employment. Regular, full-time employment at a single job was exceptional in the eighteenth century.'

(Pahl 1984: 45)

The family pattern was extended to some degree in the case of the worker craftsman or trader, where apprentices lived under his roof and ate with his children. All this, or at least a great deal of it, was swept away with industrialization and the control and order of the factory system. But not immediately. The irregularities of St Monday, of 'unauthorized absence', lateness, strikes, and other evidence of incorrigible independence survive even to the present day. The three main types of internal contract that Littler gives as being carried over into early large-scale forms of work organization are: the familial relationships and control found in cotton spinning; the craft control of ironmaking and the shipwrights; and the teamwork under a ganger of the docks and coal industry. Although the bases of authority were different in each case, says Littler, 'all three relationships were relations of legitimated independence' (Littler 1983: 66). But what is to be made of the legitimization of this independence? Is it wrung out of reluctant employers inch by inch as they are driven to recognize the heroic and obdurate resistance of their employees? Or is it gradually withdrawn as the employers pursue, with infinite patience and cunning, the ultimate goal of complete control as the last resistance to it is overcome? The evidence suggests that neither of these grand evolutionary conspiracies, either of the working class on the one hand or of the capitalist on the other, is likely. The case is rather that control, as an absolute ideal or a goal that more or less sufficiently explains employer and managerial strategy, is weak and inadequate. A measure of control there must be (though who contributes to it and why is a complex matter), but the measure may be calculated against a number of other considerations: the comparative advantages of peace, and a quiet life, of accepting the *status quo*, of the sufficient benevolence of the market, of the advantage of goodwill and co-operation and of the need to bank these against hard times, and of the need to preserve loyal and skilled labour.

Garside and Gospel tell us that 'it is customary to think of the nineteenth-century entrepreneur himself directly employing, supervising, and controlling his work force and dealing with trade unions', but that 'many entrepreneurs left the tasks of labour management to others' (Garside and Gospel 1982: 101). In the earlier phase of large-scale industrial employment the more usual form of alternative to direct employer control was the use of the contractor. In this pattern the employer entered into a contract with someone else who engaged, in turn, to recruit labour and to contract with it for the performance of necessary services. In many cases the duties of the labour contractor or sub-contractor went further to encompass the control, payment, and discipline of the labour. In some industries it was the principal if not sole form of labour management. In some it cascaded down into a system of engagement of small groups, as in the butty system of the coal-mining industry. In others it was an effective means of recruiting the itinerant armies of workers that built the canals and railways of Britain before they moved on to provide the same services for Europe. While the names of the great railway engineers like Brunel are still celebrated, the powerful labour contractors like Thomas Brassey (later Earl Brassey) and Sir Thomas Peto are largely forgotten. Labour contracting took a peculiar form in dock work when the union could take the responsibility for the provision of labour and, to some extent, for its control. Questions of seniority, promotion, permanent or temporary engagement, and discipline were all, in part, matters for the unions to decide, along with the negotiation of the annual contract. The union's equivocal position gave it considerable power and sometimes raised questions of undue influence and even corruption.

The labour contractors were no longer mere recruiters of groups of navvies. The scale of the operations and the speed at which they were conducted meant the organization and direction of the labour force with great precision and attention to what would now be called 'methods study'. The contractors and sub-contractors were labour managers. In recruitment, payment, organization, and leadership they intervened at all levels between the employer and the workforce. The success of the canal and railway construction programme (if not always in commercial terms) may have contributed to the belief that for one reason (the management of labour was not the business of an engineer like Brunel or Locke) or another (the management of labour is an expert and specialized activity) labour management could and should be 'put out' to an agency standing between labour and its employer.

Littler tells us that the avoidance of direct relationships between employers and employees, represented by labour contracting, partly explains the absence of any theory of general management or theory of labour management in the period of the industrial revolution (Littler 1983: 64). We could say that there was no theory because there was no problem for the employer; he had put it out to contractors. The whole question of labour relationships was thus avoided, at the theoretical and the practical level. Littler suggests that the contractor 'complicated the confrontation between capital and labour' and that 'sweeping away delegated forms of control leaves the employer facing

the solidity of his own ignorance about shop floor performance'
with the result that new forms of systematic management are
developed (Littler 1983: 83). I would contend, however, that the
solidity of ignorance was never confronted, that the decay of
labour contracting gave rise not to a resolution to tackle the
problem of labour control and not, therefore, to the emergence
of any theory of labour management but to new forms of
avoidance, new barriers, new levels of insulation. Gospel
describes the labour contracting system (characteristic of building
and civil engineering, canal and railway construction, coal-
mining and steel-making) and the helper system in which the
skilled craftsman hired his assistants and paid them from his
own earnings. He suggests that both systems were similar in
the relief they afforded the employer from responsibility for
'labour management, including the recruitment, supervision,
discipline and payment of workers' (Gospel 1983: 96).

But labour contracting declined in importance with the
completion of the canal and rail networks, with the development
of more highly trained and skilled labour, its increasing
organization by trade unions, and with the falling profits of the
1880s. Gospel suggests that the two systems, labour sub-
contracting and direct supervision, co-existed for some time,
but that the former was largely superseded by the extension of
control by wage-earning foremen. They performed the same
tasks: hiring and firing, promotion, discipline, payment, production planning, and the allocation of work. The importance
and the status of the old foreman is now recalled only in
industrial mythology, in the bowler-hatted figure with the
watch chain (a characteristic insignia of rank in many industries)
suspended across an ample waistcoat. He came to be 'very
much the master in the workplace and was the key figure in
labour management' (Gospel 1983: 98). He was, and in some
industries and most night shifts he still is, the real controller of
labour and the practical direction of the production process.
Could his emergence and his importance be seen as the
extension of managerial control to the labour process? There are
two considerations that make this conclusion unlikely. The first
concerns the origins of the foreman, the second his fate.

The foreman was different from the sub-contractor because
he took no share of the profits. He was an employee like every

other and he was paid wages, not a salary. He was normally recruited from the ranks of those that he supervised, in the skilled trades he shared the same time-served apprenticeship as them (it was an additional prop to his authority), and he usually finished his employment as a foreman, rarely being promoted to the ranks of management. We know that the term 'foreman' covers a variety of different roles and operations ranging from the position of work-facilitator to the complex performance of administrative and managerial tasks. But the administrative foreman probably developed late in the evolution of continuous process production, such as the manufacture of steel, and even then the foreman's role shared with the others a separation from rather than an extension of management.

The foremen were the paid controllers of labour, recruited from it and denied access to the ranks of management. The foreman became the classic marginal man who, because of his origins and the reinforcement of his intermediary position, was often as much the representative as the controller of the group he supervised. He often acted as an intermediary, negotiating with, rather than commanding, his subordinates. His position in the enforcement of discipline was equivocal: he had to live with the people that he was expected, by reference to the formal rules, to punish. He found the rule book and the penalties it presented inflexible and incapable of the sort of adjustments he felt to be necessary in dealing with the realities of production demands and the infinite differences between the personalities of workers. It was the foreman who perceived and made adjustments in the blindness of bureaucratic rules and processes. When he did take disciplinary decisions he was sometimes 'let down' as those decisions were overturned by submission to a central personnel department or to an appeals procedure introduced to assure consistency and fairness. The result was that the foreman frequently withdrew from the exercise of discipline. He had, by then, been stripped of the responsibility for hiring as well as firing.

Littler suggests that 'the traditional foreman's power started to be modified almost as soon as it had emerged from the decay of internal contract' (Littler 1983: 87). The modification proceeded by way of the increasing subdivision of the foreman's role, with specialized responsibility for quality control, feed and speed, and rate-fixing. The development of payment by results and other complex forms of premium bonus systems demanded the recording of work and materials and the development of large time-study and wages departments. The increasing complexity of wage payments systems required, in turn, the closer control of the negotiation of rates and the development of more complex wage agreements in which errors or indulgences were costly. The unions and the labour departments negotiated in areas where the foremen had once exercised their judgement and arrived at informal understandings with their groups. The functions of labour control that the foremen had exercised were dispersed in all directions by the development of managerial specialisms, by central control of wages, by union negotiation, and, finally perhaps, by employee participation and consultation. The foreman solved his considerable problem of role conflict and divided loyalty, of being the absorber of the conflicting interests at which he is the centre and the conflicting objectives of management, by re-attaching himself to labour. Child and Partridge observe that it is reasonable to see 'that the major break in the vertical structure of British companies today [occurs] between shop-floor supervision and management proper, rather than between supervision and shopfloor' (Child and Partridge 1982: 137). They conclude that, although management may not have lost their supervisors' commitment to its goals, 'the problems supervisors face, which are in large measure of management's making, have become sufficiently severe as to place serious strain upon the future commitment of supervisors' (Child and Partridge 1982: 192).

The employers and their managers, then, are left with the problem of control. The next approach to be adopted is, once again, a version of insulation, a further alternative to direct intervention.

Associations of employers date back certainly to the eighteenth century and were commonplace in many industries by the early part of the nineteenth century. But it was the 'new unionism' of the 1890s that spread unionism to unorganized industries and introduced to them a degree of unusual militancy which in turn led to new developments among employers and to the formation of some of the major employer's federations. The federations engaged, in varying degrees, in the formulation and execution of central strategies for dealing with trade unions and sometimes for destroying them. 'Elsewhere the outcome was not the destruction of trade unions, but the hastening of new developments in collective bargaining' (Clegg 1970: 24). The culmination in some industries was the construction of central-ized, industry-wide bargaining procedures and national wage agreements and even wage structures. Employers organizations were major contributors to the characteristic pattern of British industrial relations and to the national, industry-wide patterns of bargaining over wages and conditions. From an earlier concern to provide defences against union actions directed at the individual employer, the employers' associations took over a large part of the responsibility for the direction of industrial relations on behalf of the employer. In some industries, notably engineering, a host of employers simply followed the arrange-ments made by negotiation between the Engineering Employers' Federation and the unions. And it is significant that the most clearly articulated conflict over managerial rights to be conducted in Britain was fought out over some eighty years by the Employers' Federation.

The engineering employers' claim to enjoy inherent managerial rights ran into the engineering craftsmen's 'claim to property rights in their jobs and in their skill'. The employers insisted that this 'right' entitled them to make any change in working practice, which might then be contested through the disputes procedure while the new arrangement stood. The unions claimed that while procedure handled the proposal to change, the original conditions, the *'status quo'*, should prevail until agreement was reached. The argument continued in a context of de-skilling and dilution (at least in the First World War) and reached a crisis, in 1922, after a damaging dispute and lock-out of the engineering union. It persisted through boom and slump; while the prevailing economic conditions altered the actual response of the parties to each other's behaviour at shop-floor level it made little or no difference to the formal positions that they adopted about each other's 'rights'. The argument culminated, at least for the present, in the negotiation of a new procedure agreement in 1976. The formal acknowledgement or surrender of rights, whatever the practical position, was important enough to be a major problem in the engineering industry from 1896 to 1976. The explanation must include the craftsmen's traditional insistence upon job control, control of entry by apprenticeship, and the defence of skill demarcations and status. It may also include the established practice that the beginnings of the supervisory systems (the craft foreman) in engineering resided in senior craftsmen, so that the craftsmen invaded, if only to a limited extent, the managerial hierarchy. Storey suggests that concern over de-skilling, dilution, the employment of non-unionists, and the spread of non-skilled machine work meant that there was 'an attempt by the Amalgamated Society of Engineers to claim "ownership rights in the job" on the basis of custom. Conversely, the employers claimed freedom to act in relation to these machines on the basis of ownership rights vested in property' (Storey 1983: 106).

The special characteristics of the engineering industry may explain why the singular issue of managerial rights has not been a particularly contentious issue elsewhere in British industrial relations. It may have been an issue in the coal-mining dispute of 1984, over the procedure for colliery closure, but the position of the union was so inchoate and the surrounding mythology is likely to become so clotted that the matter may remain impenetrable. For the rest, what is to be done and by what means is not a question normally settled by reference to agreed rights (about which, as Storey says, British unions are likely to be ambivalent) but by practical accommodations determined by reference to custom and practice, tempered by a pragmatic acknowledgement of where, in the particular circumstances, power lies. Indeed, as Brown demonstrates, the respect for custom and practice in British industrial relations resides precisely in the fact that it avoids the parties taking up positions about their rights and therefore alleviates the unique difficulties that beset the engineering industry for so long (Brown 1972: 45).

A very different case is to be seen in the shoe-manufacturing industry. The overriding impression here is of industrial peace, order, and stability. It is produced largely as a result of the acknowledged primacy of the national and local machinery for the determination of wages by the employers' association (the British Footwear Manufacturers' Federation and its local associations) and the National Union of Footwear, Leather, and Allied

Trades.The industry's procedural commitment to arbitration is so strong as virtually to amount to a no-strike agreement.

> 'Whatever the difficulties of reaching agreement on short-run issues they are relatively small when compared with the constancy of the overall forms, levels and structure of bargaining. This constancy has, in footwear, given institutional security to the parties.'
>
> (Goodman *et al*. 1977: 100)

The 'institutional peace' of the industry results from a mutual respect amounting almost to the joint management of industrial relations. It exists in an industry with many special features: a highly segmented market faced with severe foreign competition, and a high proportion of small family employers, many of whom have retained a distinctly paternalist outlook. The central control of industrial relations by the employers' association means that

> 'the extent of what might be called professional management was limited, in the sense for example of the utilisation of sophisticated management techniques (in relation to planning and costing, etc.), management training, or experience in other companies or other industries.'
>
> (Goodman *et al*. 1977: 153)

The Donovan Commission was critical of employers' associations for their lack of authority, irrelevance, and failure to innovate: 'a factory agreement can assist competent managers, many current industry-wide agreements have become a hindrance to them' (Donovan 1968: 262). Donovan recommended that the role of employers' associations should be largely advisory, to 'provide advice to members, many of whom are at present poorly equipped for the purpose, on the negotiation of their own agreements' (Donovan 1968: 153). Thereafter, it became almost fashionable to criticize the employers' associations, none more heavily than the engineers, and, since then and largely for quite different reasons, the plant and the company have become much more the focus of collective bargaining. How far this change is the result of the recession, which no longer requires employers to defend themselves against weakened trade unions, remains to be seen. How far it is fair to blame the employers' associations for whatever is deemed to be wrong with industrial relations is also questionable. Without the order, experience, stability, and mutual respect that is characteristic of some industry-wide negotiations, the individual employers might have done far worse. It may be the acknowledgement of their own incompetence that drove them to construct this intermediary level. For whatever reason, there can be little doubt that the outcome has been to insulate both owners and their managers from contact with unions.

But contact with workers was impossible to avoid. The result of the informal, unregulated arrangement of pay and conditions in some industries was precisely the disorder in collective bargaining of which Donovan complained, conducted and controlled to some extent by their foreman, who had been left, like a rear-guard, on the other side of the frontier they were expected to defend. Blame for the consequence can be attributed to the foreman no more than to the employers' associations; both were chosen to conceal the shortcomings of employers and managers. In order to understand the practical measures that were arrived at in the place of work, to fill the gap left by the distant influence of the association and often controlled or resisted by foremen, we must look at the practice of management control in more detail.

Littler tells us that there were three sources for the emergence of the systematic management movement: the development of formal organization based primarily on the railway industry; the shop management movement based on the metal-working and mechanical engineering industries; and cost accountancy (Littler 1983: 174). The movement had greater influence in the USA than in Great Britain because the higher wages of the former provided a greater incentive for effective management and for the control of labour costs, and because the large American corporations had created a framework of more effective 'professional' management. Littler also suggests that the absence of any systematic theory of management in Britain made it difficult to substitute the new forms of management for older styles. So the foreman was able to provide a 'rumbling resistance' to Taylorism and bureaucratization throughout the inter-war period, 'a source of opposition which occasionally united with workers' resistance' (Littler 1983: 159).

The scientific elements of Taylor's system are generally familiar, at least in outline. The more social, even philosophical elements have been largely forgotten. Taylor believed that the application of his methods would not only increase production and efficiency, they would alleviate the necessity, perfectly understandable faced with poor management, for labour and unions to defend themselves against lay-offs by the restriction of output and other protective devices. His system, he said,

> 'involves a complete mental revolution on the part of the working men . . . as to their duties toward their work, toward their fellow men, and toward their employers. And it involves the equally complete mental revolution on the part of those on the management's side.'
>
> (Taylor 1911: 27)

He envisaged a delicate and efficient dovetailing of the tasks and responsibilities of labour and of management in which management analyses and organizes the work in the most efficient fashion and then 'serves' the workman, acts as their helpers, and is severely criticized by them if it makes mistakes. It is for these reasons that Taylor saw his system as providing the outline of a true democracy.

It is also for these reasons that it did not work or, more precisely, that it was never fully adopted. It is not possible to imagine proposals that more clearly contrast and distinguish the formal objectives of the manager from considerations of his interest and status. The two are not often distinguished; indeed, they are usually elided so that the interests of the organization, its corporate goals, or whatever, are presented as the manager's own. The pursuit of the organization's goals thus legitimizes his own activity and justifies his status because they are claimed to be coincidental. In fact, this is often not the case. The reaction to and the rejection of Taylorism has been explained on two grounds. The first concerned a moral anxiety that it would treat workmen like soulless appendages; this came, for the most part, from enlightened employers like Cadbury or from professional engineers. The second involved a reluctance to abandon the appearance of authority, to step down into a truly democratic relationship, a refusal to regain control by sharing it.

Taylor complained that management merely tinkered with his system, applying the more mechanistic parts of it without ever adapting its overriding philosophy. This was particularly true in Britain. While scientific management succeeded in almost destroying the remains of paternalist employment policies (and certainly in destroying completely their intellectual reputation among management theorists), it did so 'without a context of ideological underpinning' (Littler 1983: 180). The initial application of techniques of measurement and control and the preference, Littler tells us, for the less ideologically worrying techniques of the Bedaux system, led in turn to entrenched job regulation by trade unions; 'the bureaucratisation of the employment relationship has (partly) been a union attempt to exercise leverage on hiring, firing and promotions, and to fight off the commodification of labour' (Littler 1983: 195). For these reasons, while scientific management and its apparatus of detailed control appears, at last, as an opportunity for the employer to wrestle with the 'stolidity of his own ignorance' about labour, it remains one more instance of the employer's refusal to engage in a relationship and of his preference for insulation. Rather than join labour in an equal subservience to production, efficiency, and profit, management relies upon technique, makes it the special responsibility of departments of methods or time-and-motion study, and contributes to the mindless pursuit of more mindless kinds of work.

Scientific management, never completely accepted or applied, introduced incompletely without any broad theoretical understanding or explanation, succeeded in destroying by its tough-minded approach the remains of moral concern. It may even be, as its development more or less coincided with the emergence of welfare management, that it contributed to the creation of that incubus, the bureaucratization of care represented in the welfare department.

The welfare departments grew into the departments of personnel management. The story is familiar and has been told elsewhere (Niven 1967). The development of the personnel function would appear to be an acknowledgement of the great importance of human resources to the success of the business enterprise. The large personnel department has developed well beyond the stage at which it was responsible for record-keeping and the specialist skills of recruitment, training, negotiation, and payment, important though those activities are. The personnel department is now responsible for the arcane influence over organizational design and development, the maintenance of job enrichment, performance appraisal, and management development. The organization is also encouraged to look to its personnel department for help in the formulation of employment policies, even for an employment philosophy. Here at last, then, is the employing organization grasping the nettle of employment and articulating a practical and theoretical approach to the problems of labour management.

This brief account is very much as some personnel managers would like to see it, but reality may be different. There is an almost uninterrupted tradition of criticism of the personnel management function, on grounds of its irrelevance to the organization's goal (Petrie 1965), to business (Fogarty 1963; Drucker 1968), of its lack of status (Herman 1968; Crichton 1968), and its ineffectiveness (Legge 1978). Legge, while suggesting ways in which its contribution can be effectively directed by the acquisition of power and influence in organizations, also suggests that its position is rather paradoxical because it can have no indices of success for itself outside areas of performance that are the responsibility of other functional departments. So that, for example, if its recruitment and selection of sales staff improves it is the Sales Department that gets the congratulations.

There are a host of such practical problems but the one that concerns us here is particular to the relationship between the personnel manager and the 'line' manager whom he advises. The classic account of this much-discussed problem is that all managers must exercise ultimate responsibility for personnel management, but they will exercise it better if they listen to the advice of their functional specialists from the personnel department. But the heart of the problem of the relationship is that they don't seek the advice, they don't respect it, and they don't take it. The result is that, as Legge puts it,

'although the personnel department may be responsible for the design of various "personnel" programmes or systems (e.g. job evaluation, management appraisal, wage and salary structure), their implementation must not only take place within other management systems, but largely involve the managers of those systems. Hence, the success or failure of a personnel programme, even within its own terms, is often removed from the direct control of the personnel specialists themselves.

(Legge 1978: 65)

Legge goes on to point out that appraisal schemes frequently founder because line managers are reluctant to put the time and effort into them to make them work. She concludes that such problems are the result of the personnel managers' lack of expertise, influence, and power.

But they could be the result of a quite different cause and a failure to understand the true nature of the relationship between the line manager and his personnel specialist. What if the personnel department's function is something like that of the sacrificial goat that carries the sins of its people into the wilderness? The goat, no doubt, deserves a certain gratitude, but relationships with it are not likely to be close and co-operative. The personnel department may not only be the repository of administrative chores that no one else can be bothered with (as Drucker believed); it may also be the performer of certain necessary functions, basic but vital, that others see as demeaning. Such an explanation is not unlikely for the industrial relations aspect of personnel management. The Donovan Report pointed out that there were more than 10,000 personnel managers in industry (there are over 25,000 today) and that the scope of the job had vastly increased. Why then, it innocently asked, 'if companies have their own personnel specialists . . . have they not introduced effective personnel policies to control methods of negotiations and pay structures within their firms?'. And then, in addressing the question, the Report seemed to imply that the explanation lay in the existence of these same personnel managers: 'Many firms have no such policy, and perhaps no conception of it. They employ a personnel officer to be responsible for certain tasks' (Donovan 1968: 25).

The drift of this reasoning certainly contradicts the conclusion reached by the Donovan Commission, that it would be effective to incorporate the personnel management function at board level. But that recommendation, vain though it might have been, was intended to bring home to senior management of companies their own direct responsibility for personnel matters. The proposal fails against the bureaucratic fallacy that responsibility, to be recognized as important, must be placed under the control of a specialized agency. In the case of the personnel function the likely explanation is not that the personnel managers fail through lack of influence or understanding of their role, it is rather that they have been appointed so that management can escape from any responsibility for its exercise. Selection, appraisal, training, negotiation can all be seen as aspects of management that are irritating, tiresome, or embarrassing, and, therefore, as responsibilities of the personnel department. If that is the case it is not surprising that line managers refuse to support or understand the personnel department – they have created it to avoid disturbing their own ignorance. Personnel departments are monuments to the refusal of managers to recognize their responsibility for labour.

I have argued that the interpretation that sees management as moving with inexorable logic from one strategy of control to another is mistaken. It is, at the very least, a gross oversimplification to set out from a market perspective and to see management as the rational instrument for the pursuit of economic goals. It is equally naïve, from a Marxist perspective, to see management as the mindless agent of capitalism restlessly striving for the single goal of the efficient extraction of surplus labour. Each explanation shows the errors of oversimplification concerning the identity and unity of the group that it explains, and of naïveity concerning the significance of rationality in its motivation. Each account rests uneasily upon the foundation of functional determinism. The astonishing persistence of each of those myths as explanations of managerial behaviour may rest, in part, upon the utility of the myth for managers themselves. The attribution of God-like omniscience, even by your enemies, must be quite comforting. It may be that this is why the functionary explanation is now being challenged more vigorously within the Marxist camp than in the market. The theoretical crisis on the left seems to have been created by

Braverman's work, at first hailed as 'seminal', and then seen to be embarrassing in the unassailable power that it imputed to management as the blind, determined functionary of capital (Braverman 1974). Whatever the motivation for the discussion that Braverman's thesis provoked, the outcome has been the quite proper conclusion that he was, in this respect, wrong.

The case is well put by Salaman who says that

'the evidence is that the development of strategies of control has been sporadic, muddled, and intermittent, with some periods of achievement, followed by others of failure, and with managers varying in their receptivity to new systems (managers in this country being notoriously slow at accepting the innovation of their North American counterparts).'

(Salaman 1982: 57)

It is incorrect to argue that systems of work control are simply reflexes determined by the overriding system of monopoly capitalism, although they are not completely detached from it. The control system is, says Salaman, more complex, more contradictory, and more autonomous because the responses of management are influenced by their own ignorance, 'their own structures of knowledge and perception; their own sectional interests and objectives' (Earl 1983: 127). Interests and objectives will reflect, among other features, the position of managers in the organizational hierarchy (the perspective of a shift super-visor is likely to be very different from a director), functional specialism, and professional attachment to colleagues with values that may be different from those of the employing organization. Some of the manager's ideas may be held because they are useful to him in legitimating his position, not because they enable him to exercise control (Child's distinction between the legitimating and technical function of managerial ideology). In this respect there is an argument, from Earl and others, that even the theories and routines of technical and administrative control, even the unassailable precision of accountancy, serve a mythical and legitimatory purpose:

'This accounting rhetoric, by its apparently clear, fundamental, and unarguable expression of organisational ends and means is particularly suited for justification and legitimation of actual or potential political power and exchange relationships, with their inherent contradictions that cannot be openly admitted or in many cases resolved.'

(Earl 1983: 127)

The fact that this view seems, at first sight, to be unlikely and untenable, is a measure of the success of the language of control and management science that constructs impenetrable barriers of rhetoric to convince us and the managers that they know what they are doing and should be obeyed.

In distinguishing between the technical and legitimating functions of management thought, Child says that the latter is directed at securing social recognition and approval for managerial authority and the way in which it is used (Child *et al.* 1983: 22). But it may be that the technical aspects also contribute to the securing of social recognition and approval. And if the technical content does not itself rest upon an apparatus of scientific theory, then its claims to do so are 'rhetorical', 'mythical', and 'ideological' in their intention. In other words, *all* management thought is legitimatory and most of it would seem to be deceptively so. Let us examine this possibility further.

The 'ideological' aspect of managerial claims that subordinates should do what they are told to do is familiar. Ideological justification for managerial authority descends from God in a singular justification for Protestant effort and reward; it comes from the social setting that sees to it that self-help is rewarded and that the weak perish; it comes (in a surprising contemporary revival of old Manchester nostrums) in a dogma that economic terms are 'simple and irrefragable'; it comes in the view that managers are experts and must be obeyed; and, finally, it seems to disappear with the social scientist's claim that a properly constructed environment will condition a response from self-fulfilled and efficient workers. All these versions of supportive ideology share two characteristics: they seem to emerge from the environment rather than from management itself and they are inaccurate or grossly exaggerated. To the extent that they are accounts of the environment they can be seen as reinforcing that tradition of retreat that I have described. Managers and employers have been able to avoid coming to terms with the 'stolidity of their ignorance' by reinforcing strategies of insulation with an ideological account that 'explains' their relationships with their subordinates in terms that do not require introspection about it. Management ideology, as has been observed elsewhere, faces both ways in that it requires subordination and legitimates the authority of those who command it. It also serves two functions in this other sense: it clouds and obscures the view into management from outside and it prevents managers from seeking any real understanding of their relationship of authority and its true foundation. Managers are prevented from examining the nature of their authority and their relationship with labour by the pursuit of ideological legitimation, which has served to obscure the issue.

Legitimatory and technical management theory serve exactly the same function in this respect. Both protect managers from the sceptical examination of outsiders and prevent managers from seeing themselves. Both are obstacles in the way of development of any theoretical exploration of management and its relationship with labour. But what if this is the real function of ideology? What if the insulation of management from contact with labour is reflected in its theoretical isolation from criticism? Surely, in these circumstances, managers enjoy the protection claimed by any priesthood, of constructing its own epistemology, a theory of knowledge disseminated by the priests that reinforces their central role. If this is the case, why should they permit, much less encourage, the destruction of their intellectual cocoon? The question takes us back to the distinction we made to begin with, between governmental theory and legitimatory theory. If the latter is directed at 'securing social recognition and approval' for managerial authority, governmental theory is concerned to explain rather than secure that approval, it is a theory of the relationship of authority in management, not a defence, much less an obfuscation of it. The governmental theory of management is, like political theory, a search for an explanation rather than a disguise. And the explanation for the necessity for management to engage in the construction of governmental theory is the fact that the legitimatory alternative will not suffice, a truth the evidence for which lies in the fact of the present discussion and those others to which it relates. More precisely, all the evidence available suggests that legitimatory theory does not secure legitimation. Its constant pursuit guarantees for managers only the perpetuation of that stolid ignorance, their refusal to examine their world and their position in it. The result is the continuing absence of any explanation of management, the continuing cynicism of labour concerning management's role, and the allegation that management's sole skill is histrionic. Legitimatory theory searches for and finds phantasms; while they are mistaken for reality they will prevent the investigation of more material questions.

For the moment all that managers have to support them is myth because that is all that they have looked for. I have suggested that even the most 'scientific' apparatus of control techniques can be seen as a part of that tradition of rational control that is beginning to be seen as a supporting myth. It would seem more plausible to explain the behaviour of managers as a succession of retreats from control caused by the continuous unmasking of their legitimatory devices. Such an explanation seems to be at least as tenable as the orthodoxy that opposes it. If the explanation is accepted then it must be time for management to stand and fight, or at least to sit and think, however painful the process might be.

In the meantime, the alternative is summarized with admirable clarity by John Storey. After referring to Dahrendorf's description of managers as 'unwilling' rulers and to the early factory owners' preference for relying on labour contracting, he quotes a modern textile plant manager: 'I don't want to watch over these people. I mean I don't actually enjoy it you know. In fact, the whole of that side of business is no bloody fun at all' (Storey 1983: 127).

5
The education of
managers

There are three contiguous areas to be examined: management education, management training, and management development. They may be broadly distinguished by regarding management education as preparatory to a career in management and as taking place outside it in educational institutions of various kinds: university business schools, universities, polytechnics, technological colleges, and the like. Education is believed to provide theoretical or conceptual learning with the addition of some analytic skills so that the potential manager is the better equipped to synthesize the experience he gets and the more quickly reach levels of senior management for which he is supposed to be prepared. Management training is likely to be provided by or within the employing organization, to be more concerned with the provision of skills and techniques that have been identified as relevant by the organization's appraisal programmes, and to be provided at stages believed to be appropriate to the manager's potential and the organization's needs. It is thus frequently entitled 'middle' or 'senior' or designated in terms of the particular range of skills and activities it covers: 'export administration control', 'cost accounting', 'safety and health'. Management development is the process of making judgements of the manager's potential, the requirement for planned experience or training necessary to realize his potential, and the assessment of the needs of the organization that he might be developed to fill. Management development may call for changing the jobs of managers to provide them with required kinds of experience as part of the planning of their careers; it might also require training courses or even a return to full-time education in one of the business schools. Management development is now regarded as an inseparable partner to, and as sometimes proceeding outside the more formal and recognizable arrangements for, education and training. Organizations will therefore claim that it is an important part of their strategy to provide a supportive and challenging context in which managers can engage in self-development.

Because the relationships between education, development, and training are close and because each of them cannot be defined with precision or analysed accurately, we shall take all three as subsumed under the heading of 'education' for the purpose of this discussion.

The attitude of management to the education of managers, particularly in Britain, has always been sceptical and negative; only comparatively recently has it advanced to ambivalence. In 1874, *Engineering* declared that it would be impossible for engineers to lead industrial enterprises until they had developed a sound understanding of 'economics'. In 1893 the same journal complained again that while costing and commercial knowledge were essential to successful manufacturing, 'the great majority of young engineers are always entirely ignorant of a very essential part of their training' (Urwick and Brech 1957: 118). In 1913, the axiom was announced 'that has characterised British industry almost to our own day', that success in management depends upon 'personal qualities, an ability to handle people and situations – on something that is inherent in men "born" to be leaders in industry' (Urwick and Brech 1957: 123). Such a belief is incompatible with a regard for the efficacy of education, and its survival 'to our own day' may explain that peculiarly defensive, apologetic air of management trainers, that seems to suggest that they are permitted to survive while times are good, as indications of their patron's progressive position, elegant dependants whose days may be numbered.

It was, Urwick and Brech tell us, a government department that first proposed a system of workshop training for foremen and managers in 1902. It was a symptomatic start for in 1984 the British Institute of Management reported that the public sector 'is appreciably better provided with Management Development and Training Staff than the bulk of the industrial sector': its average complement of trainers was 6.1 against private companies' 1.7; 34 per cent of the surveyed organizations employed no full-time training and development staff at all (Peel 1984: 5). But by now, if industry's direct involvement in management education is patchy, the provision of specialized management education in the tertiary sector of education is well-established. But it was tardy. Urwick and Brech observe that while 'almost every major university in the United States had a well-staffed faculty teaching some of the aspects of management . . . there was at the outbreak of war (1939) only a single chair at either of the older English universities, the Montague Burton Professorship of Industrial Relations at Cambridge, which as much as touched on the question' (Urwick and Brech 1957: 230). In fairness to the British record they should perhaps have added that similar chairs had also been established at Leeds and at Cardiff.

In order to understand the way in which management education has developed in Britain we must distinguish between the locations and to some extent the levels at which it is provided. For our purpose it will be convenient to separate preparatory management and continuing management education. Preparatory management education tends to be the province of institutions of higher education, although they do not monopolize it. Continuing management education takes place in employing organizations for the most part, although they may send their most promising managers back to the universities or business schools in preparation for the next stage of career development. This simple distinction will enable us to examine the kind of educational provision that is made in two of the most significant sets of institutions: on the one hand the universities and the business schools, on the other the management staff colleges.

Before we look at a sample (the word has no statistical significance here) of both the one and the other we must enter some important disclaimers. First, we are not attempting to make a balanced assessment of the state of management education in this country. We are rather attempting to describe, and certainly not to judge, the quality of education provided by British employers. Our examination of management education as it is provided by employers themselves is confined to its most visible element: the courses provided by well-established management staff colleges. Two comments are also necessary about this examination, limited though it is in itself. The organizations that maintain staff colleges are among the biggest and most prestigious; their training arrangements are likely to be the best. Some of the staff colleges that we shall be discussing are maintained by the best-known names of British industry. Because they are good, or best, they are unrepresentative and that suits our purpose. Our conclusion will concern the limitations of management education, not as regards its techniques (which we are not competent to judge), but in terms of its perceptions and perspectives. If criticism can be levelled at the best it is likely to apply, in that particular respect, to the whole.

Let us begin with university provision of management education with the same reservation that those three institutions whose courses are described are not necessarily representative.

MANAGEMENT EDUCATION IN UNIVERSITIES AND BUSINESS SCHOOLS

The authors of *Masters of Business?*, beginning by acknowledging the addiction of British managers to what we have termed a conservative view of leadership qualified only by an acknowledgement of the need to gain experience in the work place, point out that those managers have, on the whole, had no time for the notion of university education in management (Whitley, Thomas, and Marceau, 1981). While the establishment of those pioneering departments of industrial relations at Cambridge, Cardiff, and Leeds goes back to the 1930s, the establishment of the Administrative Staff College at Henley (not a university) had to wait until the end of the Second World War. The Franks Report and the Robbins Report each proposed the establishment of two business schools in Britain. The London and the Manchester Business Schools were opened in 1965. In total there are twenty-eight British universities providing manage- ment education, sometimes in separate units, like the Oxford Management Centre or Bath, sometimes in autonomous schools or departments within business schools or faculties, like Bradford or Leeds, sometimes within more general faculties or in departments of economics.

Let us look in some detail at the course content of the various programmes provided at three well-known British business schools: London, Manchester, and the Bradford Management Centre.*

The London Business School

The courses were described by the authors of *Masters of Business?* as, from the start, given to an emphasis on the quantitative and economic aspects of business studies with comparatively little attention paid to behavioural studies. The approach taken by the School stressed academic excellence, intellectual rigour, and thorough drilling in the basic academic disciplines. Two modifications were made in this approach, in 1970 and in 1974. As a result, the second year of the Masters in Business Administration (MBA) programme became largely 'elective', the quantitative element in the first year was reduced, and increased attention was given to more directly managerial or to more 'relevant' topics, like marketing, finance, business policy, and management problems.

The provisions available in 1984 were as follows. *The Full- Time Master's Programme* can be taken full-time (twenty-one months) or part-time (thirty-six months).

'The central concept of the programme is that management can be taught as a unified body of essential knowledge which can be applied to any organisation. The Programme's major

* All quotations in the following accounts of curricula are taken from published brochures, course descriptions, or annual accounts of institutions.

function is therefore to prepare men and women for careers in the management of private and public sector organisations.'

Entrants who do not possess 'A' level mathematics may be required to attend a preliminary mathematics course. The first year emphasizes 'basic management skills' in quantitative methods, accounting, economics, finance, organizational behaviour, business policy, and production management. Every participant has to complete a programme of core courses that consists of:

accounting and financial management;
data analysis and computing;
finance;
general management in the public and private sectors;
industrial relations and management of human resources;
law;
macro-economics;
management/business policy;
management control and cost analysis;
marketing;
micro-economics;
operations management;
operational research;
organizational behaviour and design.

In addition some sixty 'elective courses' are provided that fill an increasingly important proportion of the course as it progresses. By the last two terms the emphasis is almost entirely upon a 'portfolio' of elective courses and projects. Projects are designed to test knowledge and skills in areas sponsored by external clients and supervised by members of faculty.

The elective courses provide the opportunity for specialization within the basic fields of management: financial analysis; marketing; advertising; business forecasting, analysis, and policy; taxation, managerial accounting; banking, decision systems, economic forecasting; office systems; design and product innovation; international banking and financial management; interpersonal skills; manufacturing policy and technology; and others. There are several elective courses of an unusual kind for which we quote a fuller description:

(a) *Collectivism and Individualism: the Theoretical Foundations of Business* covers the role of the state, distributive justice, political creeds, property rights, utopia, bureaucracy, management expertise, the rise and decline of nations, business morality, scientific methodology, and censorship and secrecy.

(b) *Culture and the Corporation* sets out to determine what culture is, what its role is in the company, how it is determined, and how it is used as a tool of strategic management.

(c) *Lessons from Business History and Biography* uses the resources of business history and biography to increase understanding of various aspects of business, its conduct and environment.

(d) *People and Organization: Gender and Work* deals with the analysis of gender influences on work behaviour at individual group and organizational levels, with particular emphasis on associated managerial processes.

(e) *Themes for Comparative Management* aims to compare the nature of complex management problems in both the public and private sector and in particular the balance between efficiency consideration and value issues.

The *Part-Time Master's Programme* consists of three kinds of core courses: the first, compulsory, and consisting of the concepts and tools of management, the main functional activities, and the management process; the second is also compulsory and consists of national or international projects undertaken in groups and designed to compare management issues and processes in different settings; the third consists of a mix of approaches reflecting the different interests of public and private sectors. Apart from these compulsory core courses participants also take either seven elective courses or three elective courses with a major project.

The London Business School also provides:

(i) *A Doctoral Programme* of advanced research over three years;

(ii) *The London-Sloan Fellowship Programme* (nine months), intended as a broadening experience for established

managers, specialists, and professionals in preparation for senior management responsibilities;
(iii) *The London Executive Programme* (ten weeks) for experienced managers expected to move from a specialized to a general management function;
(iv) *A Continuing Executive Programme* (3 × 2 weeks) as an intensive management development programme, and a variety of short courses in finance, marketing, business economics, statistics, and the like.

The Manchester Business School

The Manchester Business School was also established in 1965 following the recommendations of the Franks Committee. It constitutes the Faculty of Business Administration of the University of Manchester. It decided that its main instrument of education was to be a two-year course leading to the MBA. It is now possible to complete the first year of this programme for the award of a Diploma in Business Administration. The MBA is now accompanied by a range of specialist courses and courses specifically designed for particular client companies. In 1981 a part-time MBA course was introduced. The following is a brief description of the main courses available in 1984.

The *Full-Time MBA Course* : the Business School says that the course is designed to produce generalists 'with intellectual depth and breadth'. It also claims that the core content of the course is wider than that provided at the other major schools.

In the first year, different teaching and learning methods are used to provide students with an understanding of basic subject areas: organizational behaviour, accounting and finance, computation, economics, statistical concepts, and decision making. The organizational behaviour course is historical, examining the ideas influencing management thought since the industrial revolution and considering the ways in which the role and objectives of management have changed and are changing. This first nine-week programme begins with the allocation of students to roles in a simulated organization. After nine weeks, students go on a core programme that incorporates analysis of the business environment, marketing, behaviour analysis and control, financial theory and management, financial control systems, strategy for change, strategic (general) management, law, and projects in the analysis of corporate strategy, performance, and mergers. Following assessments at the end of the year, successful participants are awarded the Diploma in Business Administration. A higher standard has to be reached in the assessments for admission to the second year.

The core programme of the second year involves the completion of five group projects: in operations management, management of change, government business relations, entrepreneurship, and international business. Students also have to take two optional subjects from a range that includes: creative problem solving, innovation, marketing management, strategic management, comparative industrial relations, corporate modelling, corporate financial management, cybernetics and management control, design and corporate performance, British industrial relations, international business finance, international and corporate banking, integrating published Reports and Accounts, management planning and financial control systems, the management of technology, operations management, product policy, research for marketing decisions, securities markets and portfolio management, and small business management. In the summer vacation preceding the second year students are expected to take jobs that will provide material for the preparation of a thesis of about 10,000 words.

The *Part-Time MBA* is designed for managers and intended 'to acquaint them with the latest management theories and techniques and to broaden their understanding of the issues affecting management.' The first term begins with an exercise on 'learning to live' before going on to much the same 'basic concepts' as in the full-time course. The next three terms are spent on the same management 'core' courses with a choice of one subject to study in depth from the same list of options. A further term is spent on a course in international business together with a unifying project in cash management, marketing, corporate strategy, mergers, group relations in organizations, or computerization. Students take the Diploma at the end of the second year and then can pursue a research project in the sponsoring organization (it must have academic validity, 'but more important, will prove to be of direct help to the sponsors') together with an additional 'unifying project'. Alternatively, if they have secured suitable grades in the Diploma assessment, they may be admitted to the second year of the full-time MBA course and, finally, secure the MBA degree. Students taking the first option achieve a Master's degree in Business Science. Students taking the part-time courses are required to obtain day release on Fridays for two years.

The Manchester Business School also provides a *Senior Executive Course* for people holding posts of responsibility at or near board level. The course lasts three weeks and aims to provide 'a general management overview of current and future issues', a stimulus to managers to broaden their awareness of factors in their decision making, and an opportunity for executives from different backgrounds to learn from each other and from faculty members. The participants are involved in case studies, role-playing exercises, business games, and lectures in three areas: analysis for decision and control, organization design and people management, and strategic management of organizations.

A three-week course in *Operational Management* is also provided by MBS for senior managers with responsibility for particular operations in production, finance, or marketing. A fifth to a third of places are given to overseas candidates. A project week is accompanied by syndicate discussions of a variety of topics.

The School also provides a *Doctoral Programme* of advanced research into business and management studies. The first year consists of a taught course followed by two years of research.

There is a ten-week *General Management Programme* aimed at people who are about to be promoted to general managerial positions and for senior functional specialists who effectively form part of the general management team. The objectives of the course are to 'develop habits of thought and action which are valuable in general management', 'to train up fundamental analytical skills' to the level of use as opposed to appreciation, to provide information on a broad range of issues (such as law, OR, executive health, trends in economic theory, the banking and financial systems), and to provide options to match the individual course members' own learning needs.

The MBS established an International Banking Centre in 1973 which provides a number of courses in banking. There is also a

New Enterprise Centre, a Language Learning Centre, and several research units.

The University of Bradford Management Centre

The University of Bradford Management Centre, founded in 1963, claims to be 'one of Europe's oldest and largest business schools'. It extends the range of university management education beyond that achieved in the London and Manchester Business Schools by providing undergraduate education in management studies. In this sense Bradford's provision stands for the wider range of established and successful British universities like Bath, Strathclyde, Aston, and Warwick that we shall not be examining here in any detail. Some idea of the relative weight of the three main directions or targets in management education in Bradford, at least, is given by its figures for annual entrants to the Centre: at undergraduate level – 100, at postgraduate level – 150, and at practising executive level in short courses – 1,000.

The *Full-Time MBA Course* aims to provide 'basic skills central to success in management careers', the opportunity of specializing in optional areas, flexibility for a wide range of careers, and, 'to develop the capacity for career-long self-learning'. The course lasts for twelve months and is divided into four stages, the first concerned with six foundation courses (management science, economics, financial and management accounting, marketing, production, and organizational behaviour); the second with a 'core course' in strategic management together with three 'elective' courses; the third consists of another 'core course', on society and management, with three more electives and a project workshop; the fourth stage is occupied with a project dissertation that has to be completed in three months. Students have to choose to work with an area of options that will influence their choice of elective courses. The optional areas consist of management science, economics and corporate planning, international business, business policy, financial management, marketing management, production management, personnel management, industrial relations, and general management. The choice of elective courses is much the same as we have seen elsewhere. In the light of the final comments we shall be making, it is worth giving Bradford's description of the course in society and management, the core course in stage three:

'An innovative and interdisciplinary course dealing with methods of understanding, forecasting and adapting to the managerial environment of today and tomorrow. Areas include changing technology and the challenges presented by individual political and social change, pollution and environmental development.'

The *Part-Time MBA Programme* covers the same ground either in three years of part-time study or in three separate three-month modules over a period of five years. The course is concluded with a requirement for the student to produce a 10,000–15,000 word dissertation on an approved management topic. Participants are required to attend on Wednesday evenings from 5.30–9.30 pm during the first two years. They also have to attend for a full week in each year.

The Centre provides full and part-time *Doctoral Programmes.*

The *Post-Experience Programme* provides some fifty courses ranging in length from two days to six weeks. The courses fall within the following general groups: general management; corporate strategy; marketing, advertising, and sales; managing technological innovation and forecasting; finance and accountancy; managing people, employee relations and organizational development; production management and computing; contract and construction management.

These rather tedious accounts of postgraduate and post-experience programmes have been given because they emerge from three well-established business schools, two of them certainly the most prestigious in Britain. The provisions they make, while they may not be typical, are at least not likely to be entirely unrepresentative of institutions that describe themselves variously as the 'oldest', 'largest', or 'most outstanding' in Europe. The descriptions that they provide are the platform rather than the subject for the comments that follow on management education in British universities. The descriptions serve only as an account of the kind of material and treatment offered, 'the genre' to which the comments relate; as the descriptions are of the oldest, largest, and most outstanding, any critical flavour would not be appropriate or fair to them. It is, then, to the general field of British university provision for management education that we now turn.

First, we must comment on the equivocal relationship between British universities and management education, a relationship in which management is mistrusted by the universities, the universities are regarded with suspicion by the managers, and in which each is needed by the other. It is significant that Urwick and Brech discuss the development of management education in Britain in two chapters, the first of these devoted to the growing concern with management of engineers, the other with accountants (Urwick and Brech 1957: chapters 8 and 9). The wary emergence of both groups into consciousness of the importance of management and of management education more or less coincided with the development of professionalization in each. The complex relationships within and between the two institutions, the universities and management, were overlaid by the intervention of a third imponderable – professionalization. The common goal, Urwick and Brech tell us, of the engineers and the accountants was training for management. But they go on unwittingly to give us a sufficient reason for the failure to attain or even to understand that common goal when they say that the two groups 'were unable – or unwilling . . . to accord to management its due recognition as a new and distinct profession' (Urwick and Brech 1957: 145). If management education stems from the interest of two groups each hoping to achieve professional status and if management education is itself aimed at the professionalization of the managers, some confusion is to be expected.

There are in consequence, at least three broad concerns in management education: intellectual and academic respectability, vocational and practical skill, and professional status. The universities are involved, most prestigiously with the two business schools, in order to contribute respectability and rigour; management requires the status they bring partly because of their own concern to achieve status. The whole question of professionalization is, of course, notoriously complicated and has been the subject of specialized attention and discussion. Suffice it to say three things about management's search for professionalization.

(i)   It has in part involved a search for orthodox professional
      status by way of institutional developments in, for ex-
      ample, the British Institute of Management (BIM) and the
      Institute of Personnel Management (IPM). There have then
      been 'genuine' attempts at professionalization.

(ii) It has also involved a search for broader ackowledgement
      of 'professional competence' by way of the elaboration of
      techniques related to an apparatus of examination (from
      the Diploma in Management Studies to the Master of
      Business Administration). This more general search for
      'professional' status is often the result of the manager's
      need to defend himself against the acknowledged pro-
      fessionalism of the accountant or, worse still, in the NHS,
      of the dreaded doctor.

(iii) Both the orthodox and the general searches for profession-
      alization by managers have failed.

While that need explains the demand side of the relationship
with the universities, the supply side is controlled by the university's validation procedures, its relationship with funding
bodies like the University Grants Committee (UGC), and its
own traditional and 'professional' concern with the maintenance
of academic standards.

The result is a symbiotic relationship of mutual antagonism.
Rose sums it up neatly, contrasting the belief of practising
managers that the processes and the problems in which they are
engaged are unique, confined to their own situation (hence, experience must be the best teacher), with that of the universities'
'belief in a universal basis of principles underlying management
processes, an understanding of which is regarded as being
necessary for the effective solution of practical problems' (Rose
1970: 7). And in this conflict between dependent partners, the
institutional arrangements made within the universities to
meet these contradicting requirements and to occupy the
contested ground must, like classic negotiations, face both
ways and make concessions to both parties. So, the business
schools insist that the MBA programme must last two years, not
be completed, like the American model, in one. And the
business schools and the management centres boast in their
brochures of their impeccable academic credentials.

'The Manchester Business School is the Faculty of Business Administration in the Victoria University of Manchester. Close contact with the contrasting but complementary worlds of scholarship and management ensures an approach to education which balances intellectual rigour and practical relevance.'

At Bradford 'while physically the Management Centre is separate, the close working links with the University allow it the considerable advantage of the extensive teaching and research resources available within the larger body'.

So the schools sit in two camps. But which is the more influential? Bradford has 100 undergraduate entrants per annum, 150 postgraduates, while 'more than 1,000 practising executives attend shorter management programmes'. In 1984, 50 per cent of Manchester Business School's income came from post-experience courses; in 1983 they accounted for 44 per cent of the total. In these circumstances it is likely to be the managers' preference for the short, the specific, the practical, that will prevail. This preference is not only likely to influence the relative importance of each of the three main activities of the business schools, the undergraduate, the postgraduate, and the post-experience provisions, it is also possible that it will affect the 'academic' content of each of them.

The post-experience courses are designed to be practical and attractive to practising managers and their organizations. The description of some of them are unashamedly frank in their stress on the practical to the effacement of the academic. Bradford's Senior Marketing Programme (three days, £380) 'focuses not on theory but on a practical decision-oriented approach', pointing out that 'Today the success factor in business is often not high technology or lower prices but superior marketing skills'. The account of the course on Assertive Behaviour (four days, £430) reads like a parody of an advertised cure for acne, halitosis, or loss of vitality:

'Once you understand assertive behaviour you begin to see the need to look at your life as a whole in assertive terms:
'Why am I still in this job when I intended to move five years ago?'
'Why haven't I asked for that rise?'

'Why do I always accept the dull routine jobs in the office without demur?'

The Manchester Business School, in helping managers to decide whether they are the right material for its Executive Development Programme, puts it 'more simply, if a manager can make or lose the price of the course on a single management decision, it is likely that he or she is eligible for EDP and able to benefit from it'.

Some degree of slippage from the demands and standards of academic rigour is to be expected in the provision of short, post-experience courses: in this area the business schools are competing with the staff colleges whose advantage must be the ability to diagnose needs and to meet them. It is surely to the postgraduate activities that we must look for the maintenance of academic standards of excellence. The master's degree is the traditional passage (except in Oxford and Cambridge) from undergraduate study to scholarship and research, almost an apprenticeship to an academic career. It is 'intended to be an advanced award. . . . The practice in areas other than in management studies is that postgraduate master's degrees are generally two years in length' (Rose 1970: 124). But there are two distinguishing characteristics of British postgraduate degree courses in management studies: they do not, unlike their American forerunners, follow an undergraduate degree in the same field, and they usually last only one year. Rose concluded that the general practice of awarding a master's degree in management or business studies after a course of some thirty weeks of study was unjustified and unsatisfactory,

'especially in view of the heterogeneous character of the students involved, coming, as they should, from a variety of academic backgrounds. This is not to argue against general courses of one academic year as such; but in our opinion it is misleading to describe them as master's degree as the term is ordinarily interpreted.'

(Rose 1970: 124)

We have seen that the London and Manchester Business Schools are exempt from this criticism. There are, however, twenty-four one-year postgraduate master's courses currently available in British universities. One paradoxical result is that the Masters of Business Administration, or whatever, that are produced from them have spent less time, often in a more diffuse study of the subject, than those who have pursued three years of undergraduate study leading to a first degree. The result is an inversion of the traditional academic hierarchy, in which postgraduate work has been devalued to the level of a thirty-week introductory course for people with degrees in a wide variety of subjects and for some with no degrees at all. The business schools that have retained two-year courses have done so in an admirable attempt to retain academic rigour. But even here we must notice the wide range of sometimes quite disparate subjects to be covered in two years, a range suggestive, once again, of a general introduction rather than the progressive specialism that has been characteristic of higher education and particularly of postgraduate work. The same is to be seen in the dissertation that is frequently required of the student as part of his master's programme. It is frequently the length (10,000 words) of an extended essay, a size that will hardly permit, much less encourage, the display of precision, reading, analysis of evidence, and conceptual grasp that are still the requisites of postgraduate degrees by research. In the part-time programmes, the 'dissertation' may be a managerial report of work completed, or in progress, back in the 'sponsoring' firm and it may, therefore, contain all the hallmarks of brevity without wit, conclusion without evidence, and argument without cohesion that are so often the features of managerial reports designed to defend an established or intended position. The subjects may range from the specific ('The influence of the work study department in Blankshire LEA on part-time working mothers in the school meals service') to the immeasurable ('Employment policies in commonwealth African countries'). In some master's programmes the weight of examination and dissertation in the overall assessment programme is being progressively reduced in favour of assessed course work that includes 'specific' pieces of work like book reviews, O and M reports, job advertisements. The conclusion is hard to avoid that postgraduate courses in management are designed for beginners rather than masters.

Rigour and intellectual excellence were particularly stressed, Whitley, Thomas, and Marceau tell us, as elements in the

London Business School MBA programme. These qualities were sought originally in quantitative techniques and an emphasis on mathematics with little attention to behavioural studies. It is interesting that intellectual difficulty and discipline should be equated with numerate analysis. The programmes of the schools are heavy on techniques of financial analysis, marketing, decision analysis, and the like, no doubt because they are deemed to be the equipment necessary to a good manager. But there is not a great deal that is theoretical, conceptual, or critical concerning the social role of managers. What there is lies in the intermediate area of understanding the context in which managers and their organizations exist: the law, industrial relations, relations with government. London, we noticed, provides courses on collectivism and the individual, culture and the corporation, business history and biography, gender and work, the balance between efficiency and value. Such subjects seem to be unusual, they are also 'elective' rather than mainstream, but they may represent an attempt, tardy though it is, to face critical intellectual issues.

For the most part such matters do not figure in postgraduate courses in management; the nearest approaches to them are reactive rather than pro-active, an attempt to ensure that managers understand that part of their environment most likely to affect their business performance.

If this is a reasonable conclusion about university postgraduate education, what of the education provided by staff colleges in industry itself?

MANAGEMENT EDUCATION IN INDUSTRIAL STAFF COLLEGES

I looked at the programme of courses in management provided for us (with an assurance of anonymity) by eight organizations in their management staff colleges. A general word first about these institutions. They are, for the most part, large residential centres, frequently established in country houses in settings of cultivated parkland. At first sight they would instantly confirm Professor Wiener's thesis about the addiction of the biggest and best of Britain's industrial and commercial enterprises to a rural idyll and a pastoral history. At one time some part of their educational programmes would have further confirmed that view. In some cases, in the 1950s and 1960s, they were more like managerial finishing schools than centres for the provision of education, skills, and understanding. Course members, some of them straying into the gracious ambience of an Elizabethan manor house for the first time, were taught how to behave as well as how to speak and how to lead men, sometimes under the overall guidance of a retired admiral or general. Sherry was taken (on large courses, in rotation) with the principal before dinner and the port was circulated in the proper direction after it. The courses were visited by Leaders of Society dealing with large themes. Courses gave temporary access to a privileged club, as though in promise of what might be if our managers worked hard and got to the top.

Some such elements persist here and there but in general the content of staff college courses is now much more practical, business related, and technical. This is the range of courses provided by eight staff colleges.

Management Course and Conference Centre A

Training is defined as 'a service to management as an aid to maintaining and improving the efficiency and profitable oper-ation of the business to achieve its objectives and aims, and accelerating the acquisition of knowledge, skill and experience'. More particularly it is the intention to provide for succession and to fill vacancies from within the group by 'qualified people'. More unusually, in the context of management training, it is to include 'the identification and development of those hourly paid employees who have the potential to develop into management and staff'. This is accompanied by an undertaking that no managerial position is to be advertised outside the group until it has been advertised internally and until there has been consultation with the personnel function.

The training courses fall into three groups: Introduction to Supervisory Management, Younger Managers, and the Management Course.

(i) *Introduction to Supervisory Management* (five days). The objectives are to develop an understanding of the skills of managing and to prepare people for new responsibilities in their first job in management. The content includes:

(a) man management, leadership, delegation, and control;
(b) the job and responsibilities of the supervisor;
(c) the new relationship: the transition, the boss, and the team;
(d) the business: what the unit is trying to accomplish in a changing environment.

The Experienced Supervisor's Course (five days) aims to broaden the understanding of the supervisor's job. The content adds to elements concerned with the use of resources, leadership, and motivation, courses on business finance, communication, training, discipline, safety, industrial relations, computer systems, and the functions of a business.

(ii) *The Young Manager's Course* (ten days). This includes the function of the business, leadership, motivation, appraisal, counselling, communication, training, finance, marketing, industrial relations (including the role of line management and the specialist).

(iii) *The Management Course* (ten days) is intended for heads or potential heads of functions and departments. It includes the environment of industry, business strategy and organizational planning, marketing strategy, productivity, employee relations, financial planning and control.

The Centre provides twenty-two specialist courses on particular skills like selection interviewing, work study appreciation, production control, professional purchasing. There are also courses on team-building and leadership directed at improving morale and group effectiveness. One of these courses (lasting eight days) involves a three-day exercise in mountainous country including physical training.

Staff College B (a nationalized industry)

(i) *A Senior Course in Management* (two weeks) is intended for senior departmental managers in order to improve their unit performance and its commercial competitiveness by focusing on the better management of resources, greater effectiveness in industrial relations, the achievement of greater commitment, greater knowledge and skills, and the understanding of changes facing the organization. The course consists also of committee projects on the economic environment, managing change, a business management exercise with options on negotiation, personal effectiveness, and capital expenditure appraisal.

(ii) *The Industrial Relations Course* (two weeks) is for industrial relations specialists and managers with an industrial relations responsibility. It sets out to define industrial relations, which it describes as a crucial area, of fundamental importance in modern industry. The course aims to provide a framework of concepts for analysing problems in industrial relations, giving an understanding of how leading figures in management and trade unions view industrial relations, and a structured exchange of views and experience on current practices, policies, and problems. The course consists of lectures by managers, union representatives, and academics, tutorials, committee projects intended to make proposals for practical action, and negotiating exercises.

(iii) *The Performance and Productivity Course* (four weeks) is for section managers of large departments and managers of smaller departments and aims to provide systematic approaches to management, awareness of the need of cost effectiveness, and skills in initiating and implementing change. The content includes negotiating, micro-computer accounting and profitability, employee motivation, conflict, bargaining arrangements, and the improvement of industrial relations.

(iv) *The Personnel Policy Course* (two weeks) is for personnel managers and for other managers whose job includes an important element of personnel management. The objectives are to strengthen succession in the personnel field and to build up an integrated personnel function by integrating the personnel functions to the business.

(v) *The Management Course* (four weeks) is for managers of smaller departments and assistant managers of large departments. The aims are to assist in the analysis and understanding of the requirements of managerial jobs; to provide an awareness of current thinking about management and an appreciation of techniques; to help understand the motivations of individuals and groups; to develop personal and human relations skills likely to enhance self-confidence and managerial effectiveness; and to set the business in the economic context of Britain and the international situation. The content includes communication, time management, decision making, meetings and working in groups, micro-computers, negotiating, management skills and techniques, behaviour at work, the business response to social, market, political, technical, and legal pressure, management accounting, industrial relations.

These courses are conducted by lectures, seminars, case studies, projects, and the preparation, presentation, and discussion of reports. Some of the courses end with the preparation of an 'action plan' in which course members have to list changes or improvements they propose to make on return to their areas of managerial responsibility, the plans by which they intend to introduce these changes, the difficulties they foresee, and the measures that will be made of effectiveness.

Staff College C (a large multi-national company)

There are three programmes.

(i) *The Management Development Programme* (three weeks) is for managers with from 5 to 15 years' experience. It has four main objectives: to understand the major environmental trends, social, economic, technological, and political; to examine and develop the major perspectives of management and business, policy, marketing, finance, human resources, communications, operations and information systems; current developments and issues in the main functional areas and the need for integration; the need for an analytical approach to management work. The content is divided into environmental factors (social, economic, technical, and political); background (current business positions); management perspectives, framework, and ideas; developments in the functional areas (supply, production, accounting, distribution, marketing, and personnel); integration, by way of a business exercise.

(ii) *The Business Management Programme* (three weeks) is for managers responsible for a profit or cost centre. The objectives are 'to develop an integrated and comprehensive framework for approaching the Business Manager Role' and to 'provide an opportunity for practising some of the essential skills of the Business Manager'. The first half of the course develops a general framework and the second half deals with its application to work on real current issues by projects.

(iii) *The Senior Management Programme* (two weeks) is intended 'to up-date and develop' the thinking of busy senior managers. The content is built around one or more major themes each of which is sponsored by a group.

There are also specialist management programmes concerned with finance, marketing, computer technology, managerial systems, personnel management and employee relations, organizational behaviour, and communication systems.

Staff College D (large nationalized industry)

The College is at the central level of several sector and regional divisions each with their own training arrangements.

It had been the subject of a recent review by senior management and the course design was the outcome of that review. The design included four general management courses intended to meet different needs identified at different levels of management.

(i) *Senior Managers* (three weeks) is intended to update managers in the industry's policies, to examine the relationships with government; to emphasize important management issues, to enable senior managers 'to review their roles and responsibilities' in the light of the wide perspectives raised by the course. The central theme is to consider changes in the industry and the environment and to help managers to consider their implications. The course is conducted in four seminars, three of them identifying different levels of the industry's organization seen as business enterprises, the fourth on personnel management and industrial relations.

(ii) *The Practice of Management* (three weeks) is intended to provide a wider perspective of the industry and the unit, to improve awareness of the needs and the contributions of other functional areas, to help the individual appraise his own abilities and skills, to enable the manager 'to get the best from his team', and to improve the manager's skills in dealing with the public. The course is described as action-centred, consisting of group projects involving high participation.

(iii) *Effective Management* (three weeks) is intended for

section heads and aims to help them consider the nature of organizations, the application of management skills, the skills of interviewing and participation in meetings, 'Persuasive argument', industrial relations machinery and personnel problems, the nature and purpose of government financial constraints, and the consideration of important current issues within the industry.

(iv) *Introduction to Management* (three weeks) is intended for future managers, people in their twenties, normally graduates, who are in their first real jobs after initial training. The aim is to broaden horizons, enhance understanding, and strengthen commitment. The more specific intention is 'to provide a conceptual framework for understanding people at work, to give an understanding of the industry's environment, to develop basic managerial skills, and to consider and understand strategic issues facing the industry'.

There are a number of *Functional Appreciation Courses*, on commercial practice, background engineering, finance, and industrial relations. These are not designed for specialists within the respective functions, but for relatively inexperienced line managers.

There are also a number of *Human Resource Seminars* and several *Specialist Subject Courses* for specialists such as industrial sales engineers, and specialized courses in, for example, central management, superannuation, systems analysis.

Staff College E (large nationalized industry; the College is the only centre for residential internal management courses)

The course descriptions and publications of the college stress that it is essentially practical in its approach. The overall intention is to develop managerial talents at varying stages in the careers of managers. It is 'exclusively concerned with the practising manager' and its primary purpose is 'developing managerial talents'. The emphasis is extreme: 'The College does not view itself as a vehicle for the transfer of the more esoteric techniques and technology. It considers itself to be in the business of developing managerial skills.' The practical aspect is reinforced in suitably practical terms by a staffing policy that is unusual if not unique in British industrial training establishments (although it is an imitation of an old tradition in military staff colleges): the teaching staff are drawn from, and return to, posts within the industry.

There is a programme of four courses related to a 'ladder of management development'. The four are: the Advanced Management Course, the General Management Course, the Middle Management Course and the Middle Management Development Course, and the Junior Management Development Course.

(i) *The Advanced Management Course* (six weeks). The course is preceded and followed by two three-day conferences in which members first prepare for and finally discuss the application of the course. The course is intended for managers with substantial responsibility who have the potential to develop further. The objectives are the provision of an understanding of the business environment, of policy formulation and implementation, the capacity for quantitative and qualitative analysis and decision making, the understanding of human behaviour and the improvement of skills in managing people, and the ability to deploy and develop the organization's resources in a profitable manner. The content of the course includes: the business environment (political, economic, and social), quantitative techniques, business finance, management control, business policy and marketing, human relations (negotiating and communications), micro-processors, and creativity and self-development.

One Advanced Management Course is held each year.

(ii) *The General Management Course* (four weeks). This is intended for unit, branch, and group managers. The emphasis is on the need for line and specialist managers to interact so as to form a team approach to problem analysis and resolution. It has three parts: the managerial context and methods of teamworking, specific management techniques, and syndicate projects.

Three such courses are held per year.

(iii) *The Middle Management Course* (three weeks) is for assistant managers and the equivalent level in functional specialists. The object is to provide necessary skills and to acquaint managers with broader aspects of the business environment. The first week consists of an introduction to a variety of subjects. Thereafter the content is concerned with:

interpersonal skills (leadership, interviewing, negotiation, persuasion); quantitative techniques (cost control, planning skills, problem solving, statistics); the business environment, with contributions from a range of speakers inside and outside the industry. Syndicate work forms an important element in the course, designed to improve the ability to communicate, develop an understanding of human resources, enhance interpersonal skills, improve the ability to contribute to a team's investigation of complex issues, and to develop self-confidence.

The Middle Management Development Course (three weeks) is aimed at younger managers whom it is intended to help develop greater self-confidence and to provide opportunities for self-development.

(iv) *The Junior Management Development Course* (two weeks) is provided annually for young managers with high potential. It specifically excludes the product of the industry's own sophisticated administrative (and graduate) and engineering training schemes. The course sets out to provide and refine general management skills in three broad areas: human relations (behavioural theory, management style, leadership, and organizational design); communications (presentational techniques, public speaking, and persuasion); quantitative techniques (problem solving, financial management, modelling, computing, and statistics). The intention is to assist personal development by the enlargement of managerial skills, hastening the achievement of managerial maturity, and reinforcing personal self-confidence.

The College once again reminds its clients that it 'aims to avoid the major pitfall of any academic establishment – isolation from the needs of the market which it exists to serve'. I shall have reason to return to this anti-academic and practical claim.

Staff College F (a large multi-national, multi-sector business)

The following is the only course on which information was available and it is not representative of the organization's formal management training. The course seems, however, to possess a unique character, particularly as the organization has a very high reputation for business performance, technological development, and effective employee policies. The course lasts two weeks.

The course is intended for senior general managers, area marketing managers (an area would consist of eastern Europe, for example), personnel directors, senior accountants,· and directors of research. The aim is to help to achieve 'an understanding of how the company manages its affairs, to appreciate the kinds of problems it has to solve and how it does so, and to be clear about its future policies and plans'. The course concentrates on the company's business, what it is, what it should be, and how these questions are decided and it examines 'the problems and interfaces which have to be considered . . . and the methods of managing them in order to produce the necessary business results'.

Both the content and the method of the course are different from the others we have considered. The content is eclectic, grandiose, universal in its scale, taking in a broad sweep of social economic and political issues. It is the kind of content that one imagines would be the subject of the training of senior colonial administrators if there were still extensive colonies to govern. The subjects of the first week include: opportunities in North America, in Africa, in the Pacific, in eastern Europe; outline of the economic systems of the world, the world economy, company strategic development, international competition, financing the international business; external environment, energy and the use of resources; social trends in Europe; personnel policies in continental western Europe; relationships with government; the impact of the law on the company's business. In the second week the content is more directed at planning, personnel policy, relationships between trade unions and industry; management development; the roles of chief executives and of non-executive directors.

The method used on the course is virtually confined to the invitation of internal and external experts to talk to the course and to engage with its members in discussion.

The impression one gets from the material on which this brief summary is based is that there is much less concern than elsewhere with the influence of any unifying theory on the construction of the course, less explanation of how things are grouped under headings and of how they relate to other groups.

By comparison with other courses it is something of a rag-bag, but the contents are grandiose in scale both by reference to geographic and intellectual measures. The method is similarly unrefined and simple, an invitation to the best-informed people to discuss their fields. But one gets the impression that the result may be far more open and exciting than many more 'action-centred', participative, and sophisticated techniques might provide.

Staff College G (a large group of companies)

Most of the courses are specific to particular purposes and are of relatively short duration, lasting from 1½ days to 5 days. The College is unusual also in that most of the courses are run by a variety of outside management consultant organizations. The function of the College may then be limited, in part, to the receipt of nominations, the administration of courses, and the provision of residential and other facilities.

(i) *The Student Induction Course* (five days) is an introduction to management functions involving an understanding of the importance of people in the organization, communications, the manufacturing process, the 'structure and philosophy' of the group.

(ii) *Production Management* (five days) is intended to give managers in production jobs a broad appreciation of aspects of their function, to indicate areas for improvement in performance, and to broaden the understanding of managers in non-production jobs. The content includes: production control; planning for breakthrough; problem solving techniques, work measurement; health and safety at work; marketing as a production function; financial principles of production management; human and industrial relations (negotiations, union procedures, communications, leadership, motivation, management coaching, and personal development. The course is run by an outside consultant.

(iii) *The Customer and Your Business* (five days) is intended to provide a broad appreciation of aspects of the commercial function and it includes market research, financial principles, negotiation, and 'creative thinking and brainstorming'. It is run by an outside consultant.

(iv) *Why Finance Matters* (three days) aims to provide a wider appreciation of the financial implications of managers' actions. (Outside consultant.)

(v) *Financial Management* (five days) is intended to give middle and senior managers the knowledge necessary to demand and understand financial data required for profitable operation. (Outside consultant.)

(vi) Two *Management Development* courses (parts 1 and 2, four days each) are designed to advance personal development and management team-building: setting aims and standards of achievement, using a systematic approach to getting things done, 'building on the ideas of others, the integration of project groups, leadership style, explaining the effects of different patterns of communication, leadership styles'.

(vii) *Managing People* (five days) examines managers' roles in relation to other people, problems of motivation, leadership, effects of individual and group behaviour, communication, involvement, and obligation.

(viii) *Communicating Effectively* (three days). (Outside consultants.)

(ix) *Export Documentation and Procedures* (three days). (Outside consultants.)

(x) *Management of Exports* (three days). (Outside consultants.)

(xi) *Introduction to Micro-computers* (half-days).

(xii) *Micro-computers – Getting Down to Business* (two days). (Outside consultants.)

(xiii) *Managing Change* (half-days) – for production managers: managing for improvement, opportunities and threats of change, planning, effective organization, leadership and 'managerial awareness'. (Outside consultants.)

(xiv) *Performance Review and Appraisal Training* (two days). (Outside consultants.)

(xv) *Techniques of Selection Interviewing* (two days). (Outside consultants.)

(xvi) *Effective Selling Techniques* (two days). (Outside consultants.)

(xvii) *Sales Development* (two days). (Outside consultants.)

(xviii) *Profitable Time Management* (two days). (Outside consultants.)

(xix) *Purchasing Techniques* (three days). (Outside consultants.)

Staff College H

The College is run by a large multi-national business with a reputation for business efficiency and for effective personnel policies and employee relations. The organization conducted a review of its arrangements for education and training in 1980. In that review, and in the company's *Training Manual for Trainers*, there is a thoughtful and thorough analysis of the purpose, direction, and future of training within the company. It concludes that 'a great deal of development of non-managers takes place on-the-job' and that this 'reinforces the need for all members of the management team to develop themselves as coaches of their subordinates and colleagues'. It recognized that, for the future, managers 'should be encouraged to be aware that work itself is the single most important continuing learning opportunity'. Some measure of the importance attached by the company to the functions of education and training is that its review recommended that the European norm of five days' training per annum per employee should be adopted as a standard company bench-mark for managers, and that the 1980 survey of training should continue to be made at intervals of five years. The direct costs of training incurred by the company in 1979 were £21,000,000. Finally, the company says that formal training arrangements are 'only the tip of the iceberg', 'only about 12% of the effort given to the development of our people within the business'.

The company classifies the reasons for training as:

(a) to enhance the performance of staff in present jobs;
(b) to help people meet at least some of the potential they have;
(c) to help people satisfy at least some of their own hopes and aspirations and achieve greater work satisfaction;
(d) to employ people in a responsible way – as human beings capable of growth and development;
(e) to develop work groups and teams of people who can meet and satisfy the total needs of the organization and in which people can feel themselves to be part of a total team effort.

Once again, as in the case of Staff College F, there is an impressively universal sweep to the scope of some of the elements. The programme for national/regional managers is divided by country or by language group. There is an

International Management Seminar, a series of international courses. The company has attempted to analyse the concepts underlying the courses and to work out this relationship to the development of its managers.

Twenty-seven management courses are described in the company's literature. Our account of course content is confined to the twelve centrally provided management courses, sponsored by the company's personnel division and provided at the Staff College.

(i) *The International Management Seminar* (two weeks) is intended for departmental 'managers promotable by at least two job classes in the next five years'. The course is largely constructed by participative and experiential learning, case studies, exercises, and business simulation. The course deals with interpersonal and inter-group relationships, organizational issues, elements of finance and management accounting, and their integration into a business strategy.

(ii) *The Management Appreciation Course* (two weeks) is aimed at departmental managements with limited potential for promotion. It is concerned with the roles and responsibilities of the manager in relation to people, planning, profit, and control. There are seminars in organizational behaviour with particular reference to inter-functional issues and business policy and managerial roles.

(iii) *The General Management Course* (four weeks) is for newer company board members, senior managers, or those about to move from departmental to general management. There are seminars on an organizational basis with emphasis on organizational issues, environmental studies (in the economic, political, and social contexts), financial planning, and control and development of a corporate strategy. There is also some revision of management techniques.

(iv) *The Senior Executive Seminar* (two weeks) is for managers identified in the management development programme. Areas for study include business leadership, world economy and financial investment and priorities, key personnel issues, the new technology base, strategic management, strategic and business development issues.

(v) *The Senior Business Managers' Programme* (two weeks) is designed for chairmen, MDs, senior directors, and senior managers with a total integrative management responsibility. The programme is designed to enable experienced managers to use and share their experience in exploring new developments in the areas of financial planning and control, corporate strategy and the strategic use of resources and funds, the interface between business and the changing external environment.

(vi) *The Advanced Commercial Course* (two weeks) is for senior commercial managers up to commercial direction of medium-sized companies. The course involves discussion of the role of the senior commercial manager with special reference to financial planning and control, investment, financial and commercial analysis, and 'the use of the commercial function as an entrepreneurial weapon'.

(vii) *The International Manufacturing Management Workshop* (two weeks) is for upper-middle or young senior managers with a practitioner role related to the manufacturing process, with the potential to reach more senior levels in the business. The intention is to produce a better understanding of the contribution required by manufacturing managements towards the identification and achievement of corporate goals. In the first week a 'conceptual approach' is used to broaden managers' views of the role of manufacturing in a corporate strategy. In the second week the emphasis is 'to examine the state of the art for some manufacturing issues using the valuable experience within the concern'.

(viii) *The Human Asset Management Programme* (one week) is for more senior managers 'who have not attended a significant general management course with a behavioural content recently and for whom a recharging and updating course' is desirable. The areas of study include the development of people performance and potential appraisal, systems, and methods; communication at inter-personal, group, and organizational levels; counselling and influencing skills; management of conflict; management of people in change situations; industrial democracy and staff relations.

(ix) *The Senior Financial Workshop* (one week) is for non-financial managers. It aims to provide 'a solid introduction to the principles and structure of company accounts coupled with the application of those principles to company management accounts'. It includes the structure of the company's accounts; analysis of published accounts, effect of exchange rate movements; the financing of business (types of finance, gearing and raising finance); capital budgeting and investment appraisal; management accounts; financial planning; selling-price decision.

(x) *The Senior Strategy Workshop* (one week). The areas included are the identification and evaluation of strategy; strategy and style of leadership; environment analysis, generation of strategic choices; evaluation of company resources, analysis of strategic choices; objectives, risks, and resources; competitive action and reaction; the process of strategy formulation in multi-product, multi-national organizations.

(xi) *Organizational Development* (one week). The aim is to increase the understanding of the factors that facilitate change, 'the ultimate object being the enhancement of individual competence and/or organisational competence'. The method consists of small-group work with some plenary sessions.

(xii) *The Senior Personnel Seminar/Workshop* (two weeks). The aim is to develop the 'professional skills' needed to fill 'more total Personnel Manager/Director jobs' and to develop an awareness of the wider responsibilities and an understanding of the 'newer areas of thinking in personnel skills'. The content is concerned with personnel management in the general environment, developing management resources, pay and employment costs, and 'social pressures'.

In the discussion of the university business schools we noticed a tension between the demands of academic rigour and the market requirement for practical utility. That simple distinction, like the popular comparison between theory and practice, is often unreal and unrevealing. The rigorousness of academic work is valued because its results are more likely to be reliable. The alternative choice of what is called 'practical' is at best made by men who are too busy to insist upon reliability or, at worst, by those who are too stupid to understand the methods by which it is attained. The relationship between rigour and practicality in business education would be better described in terms of a tension between academic criteria of argument, evidence and proof, and market pressures for solutions that are quicker but less reliable. The position of the business schools in trying to resolve those different demands is equivocal. On the one hand they are proud to retain and advertise a living link with their universities that can provide prestige and academic resources. The connection with universities serves to provide a standard by which some of the industrial and commercial staff colleges measure their activities, explaining that their courses are visited by distinguished academics from the most famous of the business schools and that, in this way, the highest standards are maintained. In this way the whole range of management education and training is illuminated by an association with traditional universities. On the other hand we see the emphasis, both in the business schools and in the staff colleges, on the practical, 'exclusively concerned with the practising manager', not concerned with 'the more esoteric techniques and technology'. One of the problems about this market-led orientation is that it is dictated not so much by practical needs but by the perceptions, tolerances, and limitations of managers; the criterion becomes not so much what they need as what they can take.

It is fairly certain however that a simple distinction in which academic rigour or quality is accorded to university courses and practical applications to staff colleges is unreal. Rigour will characterize any place where good people are allowed to do good work and the intellectual standard in some industrial communities may well be higher than in some universities and business schools. There is little doubt that standards of scholarship and excellence once associated with postgraduate work have been sacrificed in one-year master's programmes in business administration which must, by now, be seen as introductory programmes rather than as advanced work.

It is not, then, the site or its status that determines the quality of managerial education. It is rather whether critical standards are applied and whether the work done improves performance and develops the individual. These three ingredients, criticism, performance, and development, are what characterize effective education at whatever level it is conducted. They are not always present in centres of management education. Students, whether at universities or at staff colleges, are required to cover a lot of ground in a short time as the exhausting account of some of the programmes we have given might suggest. The content is not only extensive, it is diverse; even if the will were present it is doubtful whether the time would be sufficient to question concepts and examine methods.

But it is not only a question of time and of what it permits to be done. Management education is concerned to establish a common language and a shared ethos. If we are to be engaged in the effective pursuit of corporate objectives it is likely that the quite complex concepts of effectiveness, of corporate organization, and of its objectives will have to be accepted without too much analysis. Earl (1983) and others have exposed the mythical quality of slogans like the 'bottom line' but it is in centres of management education that these slogans and the myths that stand behind them are perpetuated. In those staff colleges that are attached to particular organizations there is further encouragement for the generation of corporate loyalty, corporate culture, and the company 'philosophy'. These may be admirable qualities but they do not survive long in the presence of a spirit of critical enquiry. What cannot be permitted is the sort of rigorous analysis that would expose the company's policies as platitudinous and its objectives as confused. It is often not corporate good that is pursued through management education, it is a particular view of the corporation and of its 'goals', generated by its chief executive and protected from critical attention by its management trainers.

Even where management education programmes are less ideologically directed at achieving the willing acquiescence of subordinate managers, they are still likely to be reactive. Even the more broad and liberal elements in the programmes will be concerned to achieve an acceptable version of leadership, human relations, group interactions. If political analysis, the development of democracy, and changes in social value are represented in the programmes it is so that the company's managers can adapt to them, engage in a sufficiency of flexibility to absorb new challenges without damage. These measures are reflections of the educational programmes them- selves; it is a sufficiency of thought, of analysis, of criticism that is permitted. The educational process is not valued in itself, perhaps it never is in the wider society either, but at least it has the appearance of greater freedom, of not being so narrowly confined to a means to the achievement of corporate ends that are to be barely understood, much less challenged.

All this is perpetuated and defended in the name of the practical. What is taught is what is needed, as defined by practising managers in the pursuit of the company's goals. Many centres of management education are at pains to evaluate their courses by measuring them against the opinion of course members, usually after they have completed the course. But such measures are useless as methods of enquiry: the intention of the course is usually to make the corporate or the college 'philosophy' acceptable to the managers and there are means to do this over and above rational argument and ideological persuasion. Managers on courses believe they have been picked for treatment that can do them good in terms of pay and promotion; they are not likely to reject the treatment out of an objective concern for the truth (even if the course had conveyed to them the value of such an outlook). Management education is not, for the most part, concerned with objectivity; it is concerned with reinforcement. Even if attempts at evaluation were to reveal serious dissatisfaction with course content or methods, the consequence would be likely to be renewed efforts at reinforcement rather than any more radical change. If reinforcement of established ideas and values is the object of management education then any evaluation can be concerned only with means, not ends; evaluation on other terms is precluded by the founding intention. It may be this circular characteristic that accounts for the peculiarly tautologous statement of intention and purposes with which so many management education programmes begin. Programmes are 'specifically designed to fulfil the identified development of managers at different stages in their managerial career'.

In addition to the methodological difficulty of carrying out evaluations by addressing questions to people who are conditioned, even bribed, to respond with approval, there is the problem of the perceptual horizons of the managers. We have seen from the testimony of Sir Michael Edwardes that the judgements of managers are not always reliable as to what is in the best interest of the organization. Their views are likely to be influenced by at least two powerful considerations: their own comfort and security (which will not always accord with corporate good) and the influence of their chief executive, whose approval is likely to affect their own future.

These, among other influences, help to explain why management education programmes have a life of their own and why, despite their comparative nearness to the point of production, management staff colleges often more closely resemble an ivory tower than do their university counterparts; they are insulated from the real world because they exist to protect managerial shibboleths from damage. A powerful explanation for the unreality and the unrigorous quality of management education is that it is concerned to protect status rather than to pursue effectiveness.

Paradoxically, the attempt fails. We noticed this when the London Business School wished to assure itself of intellectual rigour: it relied upon numerate disciplines. It is almost impossible for management education to introduce non-numerate, conceptual elements to the programme, which would be intellectually demanding and would result in the development of a critical capacity in managers. The ostensible explanation is that the managers would find such elements impractical, unreal, 'academic'. But notice that we have already enclosed the judgement of practising managers within the ideologies of their own staff colleges. Managers reject critical disciplines and concepts because they have been taught to reject them.

At other times and in other places, men educated to responsibility have been exposed to educational courses that stretched their minds, taught them close textual analysis, enabled them to engage in the manipulation of abstract concepts, equipped them in the processes of logic. That was, and to some extent still is, the way that British civil servants were prepared by education for their practical training in administration. In the Soviet Union we may presume that a thorough grounding in Marxist theory is deemed to be necessary not only because it is ideologically useful in a Marxist state but because its very abstraction is an advantage. Anyone who has observed a (Marxist) trade unionist locked in conflict with a (practical) manager cannot but have admired the advantage enjoyed by the former in the sheer abstraction of his education, that is, in the usefulness of its distance from the practical. It is the concern with the practical, with the limited judgement of practical men, in British management education that confines understanding to what exists, and solutions to experience. It is the practical that resists organizational change, dismisses challenge, from whatever quarter, as disloyal, and insists upon the sanctity of the *status quo*.

The delineation of management education by reference to what the experience of practising managers believe is relevant, and to what uneducated minds can grasp, has a further consequence. It ensures that nothing will be difficult. What management education sets out to do, when it is not simply training in techniques of analysis and control, is to change or reinforce attitudes in a direction judged to be appropriate to the organization. This has almost invariably involved some form of human, group, or relationship adjustment, brought about by preaching, precept, and practice involving the recognition of non-rational forces. The techniques and intentions range from an understanding of leadership, of roles, group norms, to sensitivity training. In most cases the content is imitative rather than intellectual, designed to bring about changed behaviour rather than skill in conceptual analysis. Those 'human' elements in management education seem to have remained unchanged since the 1960s, that is, since management education became at all widely established in this country. This thrust is very much in line with the pursuit of legitimation which we discussed earlier. It seems to reinforce the distinction between legitimation and the pursuit of real authority. The emphasis in management education on leadership, motivation, communication, effective relationships, and teamwork (outside, that is, the areas of techniques and economic aspects of business planning) suggests the pursuit of acceptance rather than the attempt to understand the nature of authority and its importance in the government of any institution. The pursuit is carried out within an intellectual framework that is non-discursive, closed, dependent upon acceptance of axioms about human behaviour rather than critical examination. It is not only the limitations of managers that dictate the simplicity of their educational programmes; the requirement that it is their behaviour rather than their understanding that should be changed, that they should take away simple precepts by which relationships can be measured, contributes to the general banality to which they are exposed.

The way in which managers are taught to bring about or condition changes in the behaviour of their subordinates by the superficial application of new techniques of social control has been outlined elsewhere in an account that is adequate at least in terms of its length (Anthony 1977: 230–57). One of the important ways in which this programme is embarked upon is by management education. It would seem, at least according to managerial complaints about the withdrawal of co-operation and wider concerns about the poor performance of British industry, that the attempt fails. The explanation for the failure may rest in the suggestion that education for legitimation is nothing more than the 'intellectual' accompaniment of the practical programme of insulation that we have already described. It is designed to prevent rather than facilitate the achievement of an explanation of relationships within employment that, because of its truth, could be acceptable on both sides of the relationship. It is designed to prevent the achievement of an understanding of concepts like authority, responsibility, and trust because of the belief that power, suitably disguised, will make an acceptable substitute. During a discussion of syllabus content with the director of one of our largest management staff colleges, the lack of attention to this area was clearly acknowledged when he said, 'the question of authority rarely arises'.

The consequence is, for the most part, programmes of management education that are probably overly concerned with business planning and the acquisition of technique and insufficiently concerned with political skills and the theory and philosophy of government. Not only is the balance wrong, I have also suggested that the treatment is inadequate. Much of management education is irrelevant and some of the rest is naïve.

I shall suggest in chapter 6 that a more accurate understanding of the real activities of managers and a better understanding of what their role could become would both require and depend upon a change in management education. Further, I shall suggest that such a change would go some way to contributing to management that acknowledged status, which is its constant complaint that it lacks. It is not the rural idyll that explains the lack of regard that the British have for their managers. The lack of regard is real enough but it is based, much more than upon nostalgia, upon a contempt for pretensions that are not justified, responsibilities unaccepted, and a level of educational preparation that marks a departure from traditional standards.

6

The problem facing management

So far I have merely argued that too much concern with the practical and not enough with the wider aspects of management has misdirected management's focus. Professor Leavitt has gone much further to suggest that management education is itself responsible for poor practical performance in business, that 'the decline of American management is closely correlated with the rise of the American business school', that 'the real source of our malaise must be the educators', and that 'just to add a little salt to the wound, the Japanese have done what they've done without business schools' (Leavitt 1983: 2).

We have already suggested that the responsibility of education may lie in its arid distinction between the practical and the theoretical in which the former is accepted as a shoddy substitute for hard intellectual endeavour. Professor Leavitt, once again, goes further. He distinguishes between three elements in the management process: implementing, which is about action, getting things done; problem solving, reducing complex problems to comprehensible size and deciding between choices; and 'path finding', getting the right questions rather than the right answers – it 'is about mission, innovation, vision'. Leavitt estimates that about 80 per cent of the MBA curriculum in the best American business schools is concerned with the analytic techniques of problem solving. In the current language of a great deal of management discussions, path finding is pro-active rather than reactive, concerned, rather than to adapt the organization to the environment of the future (remember that the most 'liberal' elements in our management courses take this adaptive view), to construct an organization that we believe 'to be right and beautiful'. 'Where should we send young men and women to educate them in path-finding?', asks Leavitt.

> 'We might want to send them to places that appear very distant from the contemporary management scene. We could send them to live among artists and architects, or among philosophers and religionists, or among theoretical physicists; but whatever we do, we should *not* send them to business schools.'
>
> (Leavitt 1983: 12)

The deficiencies of British or of American management cannot, of course, be laid entirely at the door of the educators because of the pressure to define the goals of education in terms of the demands of practising managers. It is not so much that the educational pattern moulds managers but that the managers create the pattern which then serves as a mould; the worst that can be said about the influence of managerial education is that it reinforces a tendency that it does nothing to control or discontinue. Let us summarize and examine the general case against management before trying to assess the extent to which other models of management have the capacity to overcome the weaknesses that are attributed to its practice in Britain.

There is, in the first place, the familiar complaint that the performance of management is weak; it fails to meet necessary standards of economic performance. Such criticisms have been launched over a considerable period. The extent, albeit exaggerated, to which poor industrial relations and high levels of disputes are believed to explain poor economic performance reflects to some extent on a failure of management to achieve closer co-operation with labour. The explanations for this failure include sheer untrained incompetence that makes no effective attempt to resolve or disguise the tensions produced by assembly-line organization within a capitalist setting. Thus Beynon sums up the Ford stewards' attitude to plant management:

> 'an unpleasant job was often made intolerable by management's self-interested concern for production and their own careers. A concern which rode over any consideration for or obligation towards the workers. Management, as far as the stewards could see, were out for themselves.'
>
> (Beynon 1973: 98)

Other critics, more benign in their attitude to the economic foundation of industrial society, have suggested that management's contribution to the design of production processes and organizations has resulted in loss of co-operation. One of the most general of such criticisms was made by Argyris (1964), who argued that the form of bureaucratic organization was not consonant with the pursuit of individual self-fulfilment so that it evoked self-defensive behaviour on the individual's part that was bound to be counter to the intentions and objectives of his organization. More recently, Bailey has argued that traditional forms of organization and centralized management have contributed to costs

> 'reflected in relatively visible features such as poor operator performance, absenteeism, labour turnover, strikes and disputes, others are less immediately obvious but ultimately may be of greater significance. Thus factors such as lack of flexibility, poor quality, late deliveries, over-manning and resistance to changes in methods and technology may in the longer term incur greater costs in terms of a company's productivity and competitive position.'
>
> (Bailey 1983: 3)

Bailey describes a number of instances in Europe and Britain in which re-organization of work processes brought about greater participation, often by breaking the rigid assembly process and putting in its place autonomous work groups.

A further ground of criticism can be found in the perennial

case for a greater degree of worker involvement in the decision-making process of the enterprise. Part of the case for joint consultation and greater employee participation has always rested on the practical experience of the employee and of the salubrious effect on efficiency of 'tapping' this experience and making it available to management. The Bullock Report, advocating the introduction of trade union representation on boards of directors, reported that it had encountered

'A widespread conviction . . . that the problem of Britain as an industrial nation is not a lack of native capacity in its working population so much as a failure to draw their energies and skill to anything like their full potential.'
(Bullock Committee 1977: 160)

The Report was sanguine about the problems that employee representation might make for managers (as it was sanguine about every other potential problem in the way of its conclusion, including difficulties that might be encountered by trade unions). It pointed out that policies could sometimes not be implemented because they are believed to

'have been devised without the involvement of the workforce. The reaction therefore to new policies proposed by management is sometimes suspicion and hostility from the workforce and trade unions, which can be reflected in conflict with management over their introduction.'
(Bullock Committee 1977: 50)

The Report asserted that, if employee representatives could influence decisions, managers would be able to negotiate their implementation free of any suspicion about intentions and concealed plans.

The Bullock Report was uncritical and naïve, both about the demand for the introduction of industrial democracy and about the problems that would follow. There is a further reason for not giving it serious consideration: it had no practical consequences on industrial relationships. The reason for returning to its moribund proposals is the concern with the problem that they were meant to address. The problem is the breakdown of trust. It has been formulated in a variety of ways. The most generally convincing evidence for this breakdown is the popular concern with the level of industrial disputes in Britain. But I have argued, in chapter 1, that this concern is vastly exaggerated – the strike levels do not demonstrate that industrial relations are in chaos. A cursory examination of dispute statistics for 1984 though will surely demonstrate the contrary: 26,564,000 working days were lost, the highest figure since 1979, and the highest before that since 1926. But even the most superficial reading will suggest that the explanation for this apparent escalation lies in the miners' strike, which accounted for 22,264,000 working days lost (of the remainder, strikes in motor manufacturing accounted for 1,042,000 days). Once again, strike statistics can be seen to be misleading.

But should we not ask about the 83 per cent of working days lost in 1984 that were lost to the coal-mining dispute? Explanations will no doubt turn out to include intransigencies and incompetence; the readiness of the union to put itself in the vanguard of the labour movement – without seeking its acquiescence – in order to defend it; and the astonishing capacity of the membership to demonstrate loyalty. But the explanations will, at some point, have to take account of a breakdown in trust between employees and the NCB, between the NCB and the union, and between the NCB and its own specialist departments. The tragic irony of a dispute on the scale of the 1984–85 coal-industry stoppage is the way that it contrasts the trust of the union membership in itself and in its leadership with the conviction of a betrayal of trust by its management (backed, in this case, by its government). Indeed, social psychologists may tell us that mechanisms of scapegoating, of characterizing the enemy as untrustworthy and morally worthless, may be necessary, in some part, to the endurance of such a long and bitter struggle. It is significant that the rationale of the strike involved the establishment of alternative values, so that the NCB's almost traditional concern with profitability and economic performance suddenly was contrasted with the defence of community and the consequential concern to preserve the life of a colliery (on which the community depended) at almost any cost.

Such polarization of values is very unusual in disputes within industrial relations. It is indeed a frequent radical criticism of the practice and procedures of collective bargaining that they are intended to deflect attention away from major social and political questions concerning the distribution and control of economic resources, the nature and exercise of authority, and the purpose and preservation of employment. The very unusualness of the miners' strike and the continual and unseemly stridency of the government's presence made it an unavoidable conclusion, in some quarters, that, at last, the citadel of capitalism was to be assaulted by the 'old guard' of the working class. Such convictions may have been held by some leaders and followers. But everything one heard and read of the views of miners pointed to a much more general and less politicized conviction of fairness that, by reference to the economic rationale of the NCB must seem both naïve and nostalgic. It was the same conviction that drove the handloom weavers to petition parliament and the King. It grew from the desperation of an understanding, justified at least in the case of the weavers, that they were being abandoned by a world that had valued them highly and that was about to demand their adaption to, or their exclusion from, a totally different social and economic system.

An explanation in terms of politicization is sometimes given for other big industrial disputes (Lane and Roberts 1971). Whether radical or not, they are, no doubt, 'educational' in their capacity for enlarging horizons, facilitating (even requiring) discussions between groups of workers previously unknown to each other, and gradually broadening the issue well beyond the original and sometimes relatively insignificant *causus belli* (in the case of the strike at Pilkington, a sheer clerical error in the calculation of a pay slip). The relationship between big issues and long strikes is probably reciprocal: the issues emerge or contribute to the intensification of the dispute, and its length enables them to emerge further as strikers have time to think, talk, and break the habit of going to work, so that they can begin to wonder why they should return to it and what they are working for. It seems to require some critical interruption to the production process to make it possible for people to raise fundamental questions about the employment relationship and its relationship to production. The crisis may be brought about by a strike or by the collapse, or the threatened collapse, of a work place. The Govan shipyard, the employee take-over at

Meriden, and the proposals of the Lucas Aerospace stewards' committee about a switch in production to output for the hospital service suggest that the traditional confines of collective bargaining can be broken through only in exceptional circumstances.

There are other characteristics of these responses apart from the fact that they are unusual. They are concerned to preserve employment (or, in the case of the coal dispute, to preserve communities) and they normally emerge from the work force or its representatives, not from management. Indeed, when managers become associated with these programmes it is usually as individuals joining as employees with other workers, individuals who may or may not have a special contribution to make to survival or the exploration of alternative markets or products. It seems to be worth asking why it is that management plays so insignificant and tardy a part in the examination of these questions. Why is it that that part of the enterprise's personnel that is singularly equipped by its expertise and training to examine questions of business strategy, to determine viable objectives, to engage in market research, to plan product strategies and effective production processes, and, finally, to promote policies of labour co-operation, can do all these things only up to the point when it is proposed to close the business down? It may be that managers see the prospects for new job opportunities in less pessimistic terms than labour. It may also be that they see themselves as technicians whose skills are simply to be put to the service of their masters, to be switched off when they are no longer required by them. They do not, for the most part, behave as though they see themselves as having common cause with the work force whose co-operation they have hitherto been appealing for or relying upon.

But who are the masters and what cause are their techniques put to serve? A persuasive and well-argued reply comes from Eric Batstone (1984). He reports the pre-eminence of accountancy and financial control in British companies (as compared with France and Germany where the emphasis tends to be upon technical and operational considerations of production). Batstone goes on to consider the implications of this. The dominance of financial control 'militates against the serious consideration of labour relations matters at top management level' (Batstone 1984: 70).

Financial control permeates down through the organization by the creation of cost centres and the allocations of responsibility to lower managers for the achievement of financial targets. Wider concerns of the enterprise and its performance are forced into a financial mould so that 'the financial logic becomes more manifestly dominant' (Batstone 1984: 71). Workers and relations with them begin to be seen, like all other aspects of the organization's affairs, as commodities or costs, subsumed under the general need to fulfil a financial plan or explain shortfalls in its achievement. The accounting perspective generally fails even to treat workers as a factor of production to be confined with other factors to best advantage or as a resource to be optimally employed. Even attempts to put a value upon 'human resources' from the perspective of the company are rare. Batstone examines the case of a large multi-national company in order to demonstrate the preoccupation of its planning meetings with finance (42 per cent of subjects raised) and marketing (20 per cent). The least frequently discussed subject concerned the labour force (10 per cent) which, when raised, focused on problematic concerns with over-manning, disputes, and wage claims which could threaten profits. In other top management meetings the only references to workers emerged in the discussion of redundancy (Batstone 1984: 71–2).

Batstone reflects that 'accounting systems do not merely foster particular priorities and discriminate between issues: their very language often serves to obscure certain realities of action. In particular, once different terms are substituted for "human being", the notion of labour as a cost becomes easier' (Batstone 1984: 72). Batstone concludes that the language of accounting serves as a 'camouflaging rhetoric' that establishes the appearance of logical connections between falling demand or profit and redundancy or short-time working without the necessity to argue or defend the case that has brought it about. The disguised conventions of accounting language thus serve to establish a presiding rationale, a ruling and unquestioned set of assumptions against which any alternative 'reform rationale' can make little or no headway.

To speak of the language of accounting as utilizing 'disguised conventions' is, perhaps, an unusual view of a professional discipline in the service of management and contributing to it rational and objective analysis. But Earl sees at least one of the functions of accounting (accounting *as* management, he calls it) as the preservation of this very protective view: 'accounting is a key element of the culture by which organisations (or societies) are held together and survive' (Earl 1983: 124).

The symbolic role of accounting is its construction of myth, language, and ritual and they contribute to the stability of an organization by retrospectively creating its own past in order to reveal that present actions and policies are the logical outcome of those conditions that have been created *post hoc* by the management accountants. Rather than contributing, as they are believed and advertised to contribute, to the rational, goal-directed activity of management, management accounting systems 'frequently are used to make sense of past actions and decisions taken, thereby discovering rationales and goals retrospectively. . . . This use of accounting procedures in a sense is retrospectively writing the organisation's history' (Earl 1983: 125). Not only history; the organization's culture is created through the language of accounting. The rhetoric of accounting contains apparently clear and precise references to organizational objectives and methods of control, the very precision of which 'is particularly suited for justification and legitimation of actual or potential power and exchange relationships, with their inherent contradictions that cannot be openly admitted or in many cases resolved' (Earl: 1983: 127). The myths of accounting seem to have two functions: the first, external, providing 'necessary façades of legitimacy and control', the second, internal, releasing insecurity and supporting solidarity. Accounting comes in a sense to stand in for management, providing 'the façades necessary to maintain the rational fiction; in this sense it serves *as* management' (Earl 1983: 131).

Gowler and Legge go further, incorporating the language of accounting in a general explanation that sees it as part of the rhetoric of bureaucratic control that seeks to legitimize 'managerial prerogatives in terms of a rational goal-directed image of organisational effectiveness', and as finding expression in rhetoric, in the construction of managerial hierarchies, in management as accountability, and in management as achievement. These serve to conflate management as rational order and technique with management as moral order. In the process, the latter is submerged, giving way to 'management as a political activity concerned with the creation, maintenance, and manipulation of power and exchange relationships in formal work organizations' (Gowler and Legge 1983: 198). The consequence of the various guises or stratagems of management is the creation of a managerial sub-culture in which 'ideas, values and beliefs about achievement have become reified into a totem. And like all totems, it is treated with exaggerated respect, even to the extent that a critical discussion of the issue may become difficult' (Gowler and Legge 1983: 224–25).

Two conclusions emerge. Earl tells us that accounting serves as a surrogate for management, providing façades behind which the myths of precise technique and the irreconcilable contradiction of power are sheltered from examination. Gowler and Legge add that the moral aspects of management relationships are avoided or 'submerged' while the basic values and beliefs of management are shrouded so that their critical examination becomes difficult. I have already suggested that this intellectual process of obfuscation and protection is the theoretical parallel to management's practical pursuit of strategies of insulation, in which the direct control of labour and responsibility for its performance and for its welfare are all avoided by the planned intervention of a series of intermediaries between management and labour. The construction of the 'myths', 'totems', and 'rhetoric' by which intellectual protection is achieved is partly by the process of management education in which we can observe specific examples of Gowler and Legge's 'conflation' of technique and moral order. Management education further, I have suggested, serves to blur the distinction between legitimatory and technical thought by utilizing the precision of techniques of accounting (among others) to provide 'façades of legitimacy' (Earl 1983: 225). In terms of the distinction we made earlier between legitimatory and governmental theory, management education succeeds in ensuring that a 'critical discussion' of real questions of moral authority, power, and responsibility underlying the façades of legitimation is difficult to achieve. The obstacles are necessary to the protection of management's status and comfort. They are perpetuated by an understandable desire to avoid embarrassing or radical questions, particularly if these discussions might be seen to give comfort to trade union or political critics. The situation is the consequence of a respectable wish to avoid an examination that might reveal that the emperor's clothes are, at the very least, threadbare. And it is reinforced by a not entirely unworthy concern to protect the community of management by the construction of that sub-culture of which both Earl and Gowler and Legge speak. The aspiration to build and preserve communities is another question, to which I will return in chapter 8, but we may simply note, at this stage, that it is a general concern that is greatly exaggerated when management education is conducted at a staff college representing a company or an industry that sees itself in a competitive relationship with others. In these circumstances, the general concern with community may be exaggerated by a more parochial and inward-looking perspective that can contribute still further to avoiding critical examination of histories, myths, or totems. It depends, of course, on the understanding of the nature of the community, its boundaries, and who are seen as its inhabitants.

The questions emerge, although they may not be expressed in quite this form, from two trenchant criticisms of industrial society and of management's role in it.

Alan Fox, the distinguished sociologist, has in recent years become preoccupied with the social and moral relationships of industrialized, capitalist society, and with the responsibility imposed upon management as the result of living in it and exercising influence upon it. In *Man Mismanagement* (1974b: 66) he observes that while industrial tasks seem to require an increasing degree of co-operation, trust, and adaptability to change, the various strategies adopted by management seem unlikely to achieve these needs. The application of coercive power to subordinates whose active help is increasingly necessary is likely to make them withdraw positive co-operation or actively to defend themselves in opposition to management's purpose. Alternative strategies aimed at achieving willing consent by means of welfare paternalism or scientific manage-ment also failed to win subordinate co-operation:

> 'by the very act of subjecting them to highly prescribed work roles, excluding them from the important decision-making,

and allocating them greatly inferior rewards, status and respect, it implied that it saw them as means to be used towards its own ends'

(Fox 1974b: 120)

The subordinates, therefore, returned the low trust offered them with low trust. The strategies of 'human relations', continually refined after the Hawthorn experiments and still regarded as approaches alternative to scientific management, were simply an attempt to establish community relationships and a community of purpose in a context of sub-divided labour, unquestioned authority over job design and planning, the management evaluation of performance and wage payment, and unchanged hierarchies of power. These strategies failed, says Fox, and so did attempts to involve workers by one means or another in participation by way of representation or collective bargaining: 'there is no evidence of job enrichment, as at present conceived and applied, overcoming this most palpable and significant evidence of management's failure to integrate the rank-and-file labour force into a fully cooperative unit' (Fox 1974b: 120).

In *Beyond Contract: Work, Power and Trust Relations* (1974a) Fox conducted a much more radical and systematic analysis of capitalist employment relationships. What passes for a pluralist framework depends upon the belief that 'there exists between the parties something approximating to a balance of power' (Fox 1974a: 265), so that a moral obligation to observe agreements is based upon an understanding that is mistaken and impressed by various means upon the weaker partner. The persistence of this mistaken view, that there is a sufficiently equal distribution of power as to require and deserve subordinate acquiescence, rests upon the simple fact that society is as it is, so that perceptions of change seem unrealistic in the face of techniques of socialization and legitimation, the apparent and boisterous exchanges of collective bargaining simply creating an illusion of real conflict. Thus, when unions 'take their place with managers at the negotiating table, they do not do so as free and equal citizens, but as men who have already been socialised, indoctrinated and trained by a multiplicity of influences to accept and legitimise most aspects of their work situation (Fox 1974a: 284). Pluralism ensures that subordinates accept moral obligation in return for a trivial adjustment of power in their favour. Fox's analysis ends with concern at the possibility of social breakdown:

'should society remain in its predominantly low trust form, marked by competitive sectional struggles, induced by major inequalities and institutions structured according to market values, the consequence might well be to make the existing type of industrial organisation unworkable.'

(Fox 1974a: 334)

There is an added threat, to western liberal rights and to freedom itself.

In order to avoid this catastrophe, he believes that a 'radical programme of social equality' will be necessary before we can generate any real commitment to social life. Fox was never particularly helpful in specifying the necessary degree of equality to be established, or how equal we should have to become, or whether some of us would be 'more equal than others', or whether the test in such matters was simply how much equality we would have to introduce simply in order to satisfy Old Boxer that things are as they should be. But, as the problem of pluralism, Fox tells us, is precisely that all the Old Boxers are already satisfied (however falsely) that things are roughly as they should be, the question of social equality becomes rather difficult. Social equality, in its absolute form (if absoluteness is to be the answer to the problem of introducing just enough of it to satisfy Old Boxer), remains an uncertain basis of moral cohesion because equality is frequently perceived to be grossly unfair: young and vigorous horses may deem themselves to be worth more hay than old or lazy horses and all horses may believe that they deserve rather more than the pigs. If these questions are to be resolved we may soon find ourselves sending for the management's job evaluators once again.

In Fox's latest work, *History and Heritage: the Social Origins of the British Industrial Relations System* (1985), a wonderfully rich explanation of the development of industrial relations and, beyond it, of the cohesive fabric of British industrial society itself, he seems to have returned to an understanding of the efficacy of pluralism even when it is pretty cynically manipulated.

'The longer the system continued to provide the higher

classes with an adequate approximation to social peace, stability and conservation of their privileges, and the lower classes with both industrial and political organisations of their own and some measure of defence against power, the more likely it became that for many participants the system or their particular part of it would come to be valued for its own sake.'

(Fox 1985: 438)

And that valuation, Fox goes on to imply, might not be entirely unsound. Both for rulers and

'for many trade union leaders and activists, the skills, traditions and values of a largely self-serving sectional solidarity, though tempered only periodically and uncertainly by gestures towards a wider vision, nevertheless became invested with an intrinsic merit in a way that appeared impressive (though to those hoping for social transformation, tragic).'

(Fox 1985: 438)

What Britain has seen is a 'long slow process of accommodation and concession on which her peaceful democratic development has rested' (1985: 445) and, Fox says, it must now be questioned whether a

'programme of radical reconstruction (could) be carried through without severe damage to the political and social tolerances, decencies and myths of moderation which mark the British style and which are manifestly valued by large numbers of the British people.'

(Fox 1985: 451)

Perhaps then we can, after all, rely upon our voluntarist tradition, on the good sense and decency of (most) employers and trade unionists, on the suspicion of central government that keeps the state's role to a necessary minimum. Not so, says Fox. The system that has taken 300 years to evolve is now threatened by poor economic performance and the loss of imperial fat, on the one hand, and by the unavoidable thrust of the state on the other, committed, whether it wishes it or not, as the economic manager of society, to a more and more interventionist role. This long-term, probably irresistible, change is accompanied by the present administration's doctrinaire challenge to the 'tradition' that had evolved among employers and conservatives of willing accommodation, recognition, and modest concession in order to preserve social cohesion against the awful prospects of breakdown and disorder. British government, Fox concludes, has three available broad concepts of central strategy: it can exhort and persuade to gain acceptance of central leadership and direction of economic and industrial affairs; it can enter an extended network of corporate bargaining with employers and trade unions; it can enforce, by whatever means, its policies of economic management. The first approach is unlikely to succeed because it runs counter to the persistent tradition of individualism. The second would require considerable institutional change (in the trade unions, for example) and is inimical at least to the present government which has opted for the third choice by way of 'indirect coercion'. The consequence of this choice seems certain 'to produce industrial or political strains of a considerable order' and to aggravate the political polarization that has already been apparent since the 1960s (Fox 1985: 442).

The more direct intervention of the state in the management of economic matters is not confined to Britain; it seems to be a consequence of the supervension of economic over social and political affairs common to industrialized countries existing in a tightly knit international order and, in many countries, it has been carried further. If it is general and irreversible then we can no longer look to the state to hold the ring, to provide an equable and fair-seeming framework, to encourage 'good practice' from employers and 'responsible' behaviour from trade unions. If the state's new intervention is likely to produce strain and polarization then the only direction in which we can look for repair is to the parties to the employment relationship themselves and, in particular, to management as the agent of its control. What may have been behind management's anxiety to conceal the true nature of its responsibility and power is finally revealed: the principal source of casting social relationships and perceptions of moral and social involvement. The role that the manager may now be required to fill is described succinctly in Fox's earlier work:

'Such questions concern the whole social environment within which he operates; the environment which helps to shape the problems with which he has to deal; the motivations, attitudes and values he brings to them; and the motivations, attitudes and values of those he seeks to coordinate, direct and control. These questions concern, therefore, the social meaning and significance of what he is doing. They cannot help but raise issues bearing upon his own social beliefs and what he sees as the desirable shape of society in the future. More important than whether he accepts the particular ideas suggested here is that he should accept the need to think out his position and its practical implications for his role of citizen as well as manager.'

(Fox 1974b: 175)

What shape is the manager likely to be in to accept his demanding role or to think out his position?

The second criticism of industrial society and of management's role in it that we shall examine comes from a distinguished philosopher. While Fox sees dangers consequent upon change and re-adjustment, he thinks that British society is sufficiently decent, adaptive, and imbued with love of country to provide hope of discovering solutions to its problems. I have suggested that management will be of crucial importance in any process of adaptation. Alasdair MacIntyre, our second critic, in an even more searching and general criticism of (*inter alia*) industrial society, cuts the premises from under the feet of any such optimistic argument by making the manager one of the key characters responsible for moral disintegration and decay in western society.

Professor MacIntyre is not singularly concerned with management in *After Virtue: a Study in Moral Theory* (1981). It is a work of moral philosophy and subsumes management in an account of the disintegration of moral relationships in western society. MacIntyre tells us that, as the result of what he calls the 'enlightenment project', man has become individual and autonomous, freed from the external authority exercised over him by traditional morality. The price he has paid for this freedom, however, is his isolation from the medieval and classical relationship within a social and moral network: there is now no authority at all. Each individual now speaks unconstrained by divine law, natural teleology, or hierarchical authority, 'but why should anyone listen?'. Each of us sees ourself as an autonomous moral agent, but each of us is engaged in manipulative relationships with others. So,

> 'seeking to protect the autonomy that we have learned to prize, we aspire ourselves *not* to be manipulated by others; seeking to incarnate our own principles and stand-point in this world. . . . We find no way open to us except by directing towards others those very manipulative modes of relationships which each of us aspires to resist in our own case. The incoherence of our attitudes and our experience arises from the incoherent conceptual scheme which we have inherited.'
> (MacIntyre 1981: 66)

The process of moral exchange has been replaced in modern society by a fictitious, a moribund, exchange conducted in terms of 'rights', 'protest', and 'unmasking'. The current climate of 'bureaucratic individualism' means that characteristic debates of our time are between individualism making its claim in terms of rights and organizations making claims in terms of utility. Both are incommensurable fictions. 'The mock rationality of the debate conceals the arbitrariness of the will and power at work in its resolution.' Protests are almost always a negative reaction against 'the alleged invasion of someone's rights in the name of someone else's utility'. No one can now ever win an argument or lose it, 'hence the utterance of protest is characteristically addressed to those who already share the protestor's premisses . . . they rarely have anyone else to talk to but themselves' (MacIntyre 1981: 69). 'Unmasking' is the process by which the hidden, covert motives of will and self-interest are expressed as lying behind and 'explaining' overt moral statements. These charades, in which moral discussions are initiated but not engaged in, are the consequence of the doctrine of emotivism in which moral statements are deemed to reveal only the feeling of those who make them. Hence, settlements of moral disputes become impossible except by reference to non-moral grounds. So, moral exchange becomes impossible.

These characteristically modern activities are carried on, says MacIntyre, by the three 'central characters' of modern society: the aesthetic, the therapist, and the manager. It is the third of these that he regards as the most important and the most threatening. In a world reduced to the exchange of moral fictions, managers rely upon their own peculiar fiction, the claim to 'possess systematic effectiveness in controlling certain aspects of social reality' (MacIntyre 1981: 71). Managers claim that they are morally neutral, engaged in the pursuit of means to the achievement of ends decided by others. But the contrivance of means is a central part of the 'manipulation of human beings into compliant patterns of behaviour; and it is by appeal to his own effectiveness in this respect that the manager claims authority' (MacIntyre 1981: 71). So the notion of effectiveness is used to sustain and extend managerial authority. Expertise, while claimed to be morally neutral, is used to justify authority and social control, which is argued to have a moral foundation.

The manager is engaged in a masquerade based upon a moral fiction; his claim to authority is built upon sand. MacIntyre has no difficulty in disposing of the two purported foundations of the claim – that the manager is engaged in a domain of morally neutral facts in which he is an expert and that he is able to arrive at law-like generalizations, to be scientific. MacIntyre says of the claim that it is a modern illusion in which the manager is the chief illusionist.

'The effects of eighteenth century prophecy have been to produce *not* scientifically managed social control, but a skilful dramatic imitation of such control. It is histrionic success which gives power and authority to our culture. The most effective bureaucrat is the best actor.'

(MacIntyre 1981: 102)

Against the moral fiction, false pretensions, and illusions of the modern world, MacIntyre contrasts the character of traditional, pre-enlightenment society. It contained features common to all pre-enlightenment philosophical accounts and necessary to any community if it is not to become corrupt. He describes these features first in sociological and then in philosophical terms, believing that these two disciplines are dependent upon each other. He distinguishes between 'practices' and 'institutions'. A practice is 'a coherent and complex form of socially established cooperative human activity' (MacIntyre 1981: 175) that realizes 'goods' (values, not commodities) that are internal to that practice, concerned with standards of excellence, with human conceptions of ends and values. Bricklaying is not a practice, architecture is; planting turnips is not a practice, farming is. Internal goods are judged by those engaged in a practice but their achievement 'is a good for the whole community who participate in the practice' (MacIntyre 1981: 178). External goods, on the other hand, are the object of competition in a distributive exchange with winners and losers. Practices require institutions to carry them forward but there is a tension between the two; the practice is always vulnerable to the competitiveness of the institution. Practices are concerned with internal goods; they depend upon institutions that are concerned with external goods. Practices would be, are always in danger of being, swamped by institutions were they not sustained by virtue.

In the second, the philosophical account, MacIntyre identifies three essential virtues, soon to be joined by a fourth. The virtues of justice, courage, and truthfulness sustain practices and maintain our search for the good in overcoming the dangers and threat of acquisitiveness. They are necessary to the maintenance of a community that, like practices, depends upon the fourth virtue, tradition. A living tradition is a socially embodied argument about the nature of the good constituting that tradition. It emerges from the past, from history, is conducted in a narrative, and confronts 'a future whose determinate and determinable character, so far as it possesses any, derives from its past' (MacIntyre 1981: 207).

The creation of human communities, political activity, and work were once conceived as practices. Not so now. When work is put to the service of impersonal capital, separated from everything but survival and institutionalized acquisitiveness, the practice of work ends: ' "Pleonexia", a vice in the Aristotelian scheme, is now the driving force of modern productive work' (MacIntyre 1981: 211). The means–ends relationship of work has become external to the goods sought by those who work. We could say that the meaning, the moral purpose, and relationships of work have been destroyed by the overbearing importance given to its economic and competitive character.

MacIntyre leaves us with a world in which moral exchange has become impossible and moral philosophy is derided. One of the most important agents of this destruction is management, a characteristic (I would go further than MacIntyre and say *the* characteristic) modern activity that, in its conduct and in its intentions, exemplifies current vices rather than ancient virtues, an activity that contributes to our isolated confusion by trading in myths and fictions.

Before we consider the consequence of this assault let us examine the extent to which it is justified. A good deal of the 'theory' of management, the explanations of managerial organization, and managerial behaviour is based upon the assumption that management is rational, purposive, goal-directed, and that its organization is structured so as to facilitate the achievement of business or economic goals. There is not much room for argument that the purpose of managerial organization is defined in terms of economic success and competitive effectiveness. There is rather more room for argument about the methods used to attain this purpose. Much of the conduct of managers is still directed by adherence to principles of scientific management, which Taylor said was concerned to reduce inefficiency by the systematic application of clearly defined laws, rules, and principles (Taylor 1911: 7). The function of planning and co-ordinating, the closer control of job performance, the more detailed direction of task control and specialization, the extension and refinement of batteries of analytic technique (work study, operational research, financial and cost control), and the submission of management structures to 'organizational design' analysis, all substantiate MacIntyre's contention that management applies, at least has the ambition to apply, law-like generalization to its competitive and economically directed activity. A great deal of the course content of business schools and management staff colleges further supports this conclusion. Managers occupy institutions both in the general and in the particular sense in which MacIntyre uses the term.

There is, to be sure, some argument about whether the right laws are being applied, as to the nature of the 'science' to be used to generate laws and principles. But it is merely an argument about tools, not intentions. When scientific management was challenged by the human relations school the debate, if so it could be called, was about which kind of science, social or physical, should be the basis for deriving law-like generalizations. Management, or the academics that teach it, have never retreated from the position that MacIntyre undermines. The claim to moral neutrality is accompanied by batteries of technique of doubtful efficacy, except in the authority that they lend to 'the manipulaton of human beings into compliant patterns of behaviour' (MacIntyre 1981: 71). As the relationship between technique and authority is exposed and as the predictive reliability of the generalizations is questioned, even in the more precise areas like accounting, authority begins to totter. So management sets out upon a new search for analytic skills and expertise, not necessarily so that it can do its job better, but so that its histrionic performance will be unimpaired and its authority be the more convincing.

In the latest search, management, by now sceptical of scientific theories, principles, and law-like generalizations, has returned to one of the less respectable philosophical positions – to crude empiricism. The search is now for where it works (in terms of economic performance: the goal never changes), in order to describe the characteristic features that seem to accompany success so that they can be generally imitated. The search takes one of two contemporary forms: what do the Japanese do, or, what are the 'lessons from America's best-run companies'. That phrase is the sub-title of *In Search of Excellence*, by Peters and Waterman, currently the most widely read and probably the most influential management text. The reader, presumably a manager, is warned that he may have difficulties with chapters 3 and 4, they 'may be daunting, because they are devoted largely to theory. They can be skipped (or read last), but we *do* suggest that the reader skim them, at least' (Peters and Waterman 1982: xv). And here are three not entirely unrepresentative sentences from this daunting theoretical discussion:

> 'Most acronyms stink. Not KISS: Keep it Simple, Stupid! One of the key attributes of the excellent companies is that they have realised the importance of keeping things simple despite overwhelming genuine pressures to complicate things. There is a powerful reason for this, and we turn to the Nobel laureate Herbert Simon for the answer.'

> (Peters and Waterman 1982: 63)

The considerable merit of *In Search of Excellence* is that it sets out to question the reliability of the 'rational model', of dependence upon analytic techniques for the discernment of strategic directions, and it reminds managers of the political and cultural complexity of their setting and of the importance of creativity and intelligence (along with vigorous internal competition between peer groups) in successful business operations. Its messages and its conclusions are supported (rather than arrived at) by reference to a host of theoretical, and as many anecdotal, references to stories of effectiveness and pithy statements of good sense. But we never rest for long at any point in this breathless race to establish the new good sense we are asked to accept. The book illustrates its admiration for the success of Frito-Lay (subsidiary of Pepsi Co.) in selling 'over £2 billion worth of potato chips and pretzels every year'. The authors market ideas rather than examine them. At the outset we learn that the isolation of seven important variables in the study of organization were arranged so as to all start with the letter 'S', to be made into the 'McKinsey 7-S framework', with a logo to go with it. 'Anthony Athos at the Harvard Business School gave us the courage to do it that way, urging that without the memory hooks provided by alliteration, our stuff was just too hard to explain, too easily forgettable' (Peters and Waterman 1982: 9). One wonders whether Professor MacIntyre had to wrestle with the same problem and what is the precise relationship between the supply of hooks and forgettability.

Well, marketing and histrionic performance have many things in common, not least that each must be believable. There is, however, in the relationship between a recommended approach to managerial excellence and its assurance of authority, an unwelcome paradox. The more effective the marketing, the better the logo, the less forgettable the saws; then the less likely it is that the ideas will be scrutinized by the writer or his readers. The search for excellence continues a well-established tradition of management writing: it will not make its readers think.

That is no criticism in itself. Peters and Waterman have merely demonstrated that they believe acronyms, logos, and memory hooks are necessary to the marketing of ideas to a managerial readership with serious intellectual deficiencies.

Judged by the logic of business enterprise, such works are beyond criticism: if they sell they are, by definition, successful, as successful as Frito-Lay in unloading pretzels upon the public. But, unchallengeable as their success is, since they set out to require change we may be allowed to ask whether they are likely to succeed in achieving?

In Search of Excellence is true to a tradition of management writing in giving two assurances to its readers: if the advice is followed business results will be improved and the world (in consequence) will be a better place. There is little or no evidence, on the first level, that business performance has been improved by following the precepts of general advice on management principles, human relations, systems theory, organizational behaviour, or OD. The application of specific techniques of control of production engineering, of accounting, are different questions and, no doubt, successful managers learn such techniques or hire others who have acquired them. But it would be difficult to substantiate any claim that business success has been built upon following the path laid down by Mayo, Roethlisberger and Dickson, Argyris, McGregor, Simon, *et al.* There is some ground for suspicion, to say the least, that the attempt to impose a general framework, outlook, or perspective upon managers in diverse situations is likely to founder upon two obstacles: its propensity to induce a failure of attention to complexity and change, reinforced by the willingness of its clientele to accept it as a painless cure-all. For this reason, much of the advice directed at managers may be the last thing they should listen to, even when it is certainly not the last thing they want to hear.

At the more general, societal level the case has already failed if the advice does not improve business performance. It would still be possible to argue that, even if managerial texts are likely to induce bankruptcy, they remain valuable on social, moral, or political grounds but, as far as I know, no such claims have yet been advanced; I know no management writer who has acknowledged that his advice may ruin his reader's business but that it should be followed, none the less, because it will improve his reader's manners or morals. Such altruism does not figure in advice to managers but it is an element in a higher level of intellectual attention to managerial organization. In his critical account of the development of organizational analysis, Reed tells us that, up to the 1960s, the orthodox position was that the major institutions of industrial society 'were firmly set in place and equipped to manage any new problems which were likely to emerge in the foreseeable future', and that organizational analysis was seen 'as an applied administrative science which would provide the theoretical and instrumental means necessary to rationalise the authority structures and control systems of complex work organisations as permanent features of industrial society' (Reed 1985: 99, 100). The concentration upon large-scale organizations and the theoretical perspectives for its analysis provided by systems theory, the dominance of technology, and the application of 'scientific' rationality to the control of work conspired, says Reed, to conceal questions of the distribution of power, consideration of human agency, and, I would add, any residue of moral concern.

Ultimately, the world broke in upon this stagnant theoretical consensus: American disillusionment with the war in Vietnam, the excitements of Paris in May, 1968, and the 'liberation' (the irony of the juxtaposition demands quotation marks) of Marxist theory following the death of Stalin conspired to bring new criticism to bear upon the citadel of organization. But the point of it all often remained the system; while the critical instruments were sharpened and refined, organizational theory remained embedded in the positivist tradition from which it had sprung. Refinement and openness to new and even radical perspectives was welcomed, but only to enhance the opportunity to predict and control. Reed concludes that, even after the incursion of new perspectives into the old conservative tradition, organizational analysis was still subject to a

'failure to recognise and appreciate the full meaning of the theoretical and practical dilemma of human agency which cannot be resolved or transcended by recourse to a scientific or instrumental reading of its intellectual aims and practical significance.'

(Reed 1985: 114)

Reed's recommendation for getting out of the morass, in which each new step immerses us still further ('intellectual "tub-thumping"', he calls it), 'which threatens the return of a quasi-scientific instrumentalism as dangerous (if not more so) as the positivism it has overturned' (1985: 212), is that we should see organizational analysis as an intellectual practice in which we are honestly and disputatiously engaged in order the better to understand the pluralist complexity, subtlety, and contradiction of human behaviour within an organizational setting. This will be an enterprise for purists indeed, detached from the market (and certainly from marketing: not much place for logos and memory-hooks here); *interested* in the market, perhaps, in order to understand it, but promising no prediction or precepts about how to trade in it adventitiously. This new rigour will no doubt succeed in finally establishing organizational analysis as a proper study for academics in universities.

Do we seriously expect managers to engage in it? To the extent that it would seem to be a rigorous, difficult, and disciplined exercise there is no reason why it should not figure in the education of a manager and one good reason why it should: it is close to his home practice. It may even help him in his engagement with the practice because 'managers are forced, by the very nature of the practice in which they are engaged – imperative co-ordination through bureaucratic control – to impose a series of control mechanisms and supporting rationales' (Reed 1985: 129). And if it does help him, if he finds that this rigorous study of organizational analysis actually assists him in the exercise of control, so much the better for him and all the more reason to include it in his educational curriculum. But what will its usefulness do to the study? Is its value in the practice of control likely to re-immerse the study in the morass from which Dr Reed has just rescued it: will it return to 'intellectual tub-thumping'?

The dilemma is real and it illustrates the difficulty in detaching any aspect of organizational study from the positivist tradition that was its source and inspiration. Any social science activity is concerned with the problem of order, and, even when its acolytes pursue their arcane theorizing in monastic seclusion from the world, the world will seize their latest pronouncements because there will be no better statements available from which to derive mechanisms of predictability and control. If control is not the purpose of social scientists their work will always be preferred to that of soothsayers as a means of indicating directions for managers and their teachers. So, the proposal to turn organizational analysis into an 'intellectual practice', worthy though it is, may yet be distorted by what managers will make of it. It would seem that the problem of organizational analysis regresses; it may not be solved.

That, however, is the business of the social scientist; our business is with managers and their education. Managers are controllers of resources and of other men and women. That they may become more effective controllers as they become more sensitive and intellectually informed is no reason to deride them or the educational process that has led to their improvement. The concern about the effectiveness of the means by which they exercise control, and about the propriety of teaching them to improve, lies with the purpose at which control is directed and with the concealment of its means. Managers are not the only people required in their jobs to exercise control: so are policemen on traffic duty and ushers in theatres, and we do not assert that *their* competence should be reduced. We worry about managers' capacity to control because we do not know, or do not agree about, what it is for, and because we cannot see how it is exercised. The concern about purpose is in part a worry about its narrowness, about objectives that are sectional and are not shared by, or in the view of some, are antithetical to, the interests of others. Managers overcome these divisions, to some extent, in societies like the USA or Japan, where, we are told, business interests and profits are believed to be for the good of all. In other countries, like the USSR, the 'problem' of control is reduced to vanishing point, we are told, because the purpose at which it is directed is the good of the people in its triumphant march to victory over the last remnants of capitalist oppression, or some such. In time of war, management control is given wide approval and none of us who are not treacherous will want to diminish it. These are all general instances of the legitimation of management authority and in none of those examples from different cultural settings is management control deemed to be justified by a straightforward appeal to the interests of a particular sectional interest or group, least of all to managers themselves. Managers are always deemed to exercise control legitimately to the extent that they are surrogates for a wider conception of society beyond themselves.

We do not have to take a position on which of these wider views is better than the others. The differences simply serve to illustrate what is in common, that control is deemed to be properly exercised when there is a degree of consensus about the goals that it is meant to serve: there must be some purpose beyond the end of management's nose. It may well be that this necessary degree of consensus is manufactured by management, or for it, in the expression of social values that management is presented as serving. The ways in which the consensus is arrived at are beyond the scope of this debate, although Fox's discussion of the 'social origins of the British industrial relations system' suggests that they are not likely to be arrived at by temporary stratagems, that they may be deep within a society's history and culture, revealing values held in common only when they are threatened.

We have seen that management, at least in Britain, has abandoned, or been taught that it should abandon, a paternalist model in which it claimed to exercise care and responsibility for the community of workers that it directed. That model was given up, or it became corrupted as management turned to other means. Divorced, at least in some degree if not in purpose, from ownership, and bereft of the owner's traditional claim to legitimacy (itself weakened by egalitarian doctrines of various degrees of rigour and effectiveness), the managers advertised their own claims to effective control. The direct claim for consensus based upon some measure of democratic consent to be achieved by participation in management's decision making was transparently spurious and seen as a means of achieving control rather than the agreement about ends and means from which control might flow. The claim to rationality and effectiveness sundered upon a reef composed of many rocks each of which was large enough to sink it. Rationality and effectiveness are purposive – means not ends, and if the ends are unspecified or open to doubt, worse still if they are seen as selfish, then rationality and effectiveness become means to be rejected. Then there is the doubt, revealed by Beynon on Ford and by Gallie on the British oil refineries in his study, as to the reality of the claims, as to the competence of management in assuring anything but its own status. More recently, we have seen that the techniques in which management claims to be expert are themselves of doubtful efficacy, either in their relevance to success or their greater relevance to the construction of managerial mythology rather than effectiveness. Finally, we see that the whole philosophical foundation upon which management's claims are built are themselves revealed to be shifting and uncertain, that management is engaged in a charade of pseudo-science and mock-morality in order to disguise itself in an authority to which it can lay no real claim and which it cannot exercise.

7

The real foundation of managerial authority

The problems facing management are of two kinds. The specific problem with which it is constantly preoccupied is the assurance of efficiency. We have seen that attempts at its solution are both contradictory and complex. In addition to the mastery of a range of administrative techniques, constantly extended and intensified, it requires the exercise of effective control over subordinates and specialists and over complex organizations which have a tendency towards entropy. This is the business of management and managers can be forgiven for seeing it as sufficiently demanding and important to deserve their entire attention and all their effort. It is contradictory as well as complex because, we are told, control cannot be attained by force or by the development of bureaucratic machinery: effective performance demands willing, even enthusiastic, co-operation to which coercive control is inimical. The contradiction at the heart of the specific managerial problem is between the need to exercise control and the need to achieve commitment. The resolution of the contradiction is sought by the development of a host of strategies: job enrichment, job enlargement, participation, organizational development, all of them 'sophisticated modern' (as Fox calls them) methods of disguising control as the lightest caress.

This is more than enough for managers to be getting on with, and it is, in any case, their central concern. Drucker, anxious as he is to indicate the social and moral responsibilities of managers, insists that first things must come first.

'The first responsibility to society is to operate at a profit, and only slightly less important is the necessity for growth. The business is the wealth-creating and wealth-producing organ of our society. Management must maintain its wealth-producing resources intact by making adequate profits to offset the risk of economic activity.'

(Drucker 1968: 459)

Drucker thus subsumes under the dictat of economic performance the demonstration of responsibility. This is the second (he implies, secondary) problem of management; not its specific but its social concern. Drucker derives this responsibility thus:

'The responsibility of management in our society is decisive not only for the enterprise itself but for management's public standing, its success and status, for the very future of our economic and social system and the survival of the enterprise as an autonomous institution.'

(Drucker 1968: 455)

He adds elsewhere that management's responsibility to the public interest derives from the fact that the enterprise is 'an organ of society', the actions of which decisively affect the social scene, and, in an Hegelian flourish, that, because management is 'an economic organ, indeed the specifically economic organ of an industrial society' it therefore 'reflects the basic spirit of the modern age' (Drucker 1968: 19, 14). Management's general responsibility thus derives from its defence of its own interest, its status, its public esteem, from its concern for the preservation of the capitalist system, and, finally, from a recognition of its impact upon society and of its representing the spirit of the age. There are three levels of managerial responsibility growing from a concern with its own skin and reputation, a concern for the economic system of which it is a part, and, at the most generalized, a concern for society. These are all, in some measure, defensive postures and we have seen them edge their way into management courses at the staff colleges that we examined so that managers have to be reminded of the consequences on the wider society of their specific actions and decisions because society's reactions can, if those decisions are 'irresponsible', damage their own interests or those of their organizations. So, there is a clear connection between economic activity and social consequence and it is this public responsibility of management that 'must therefore underlie all its behaviour. Basically it furnishes the ethics of management' (Drucker 1968: 455).

The ethics of management are, however, limited, first to the extent to which an instrumental concern for self-interest can extend its concern and, second, by a severe limitation of the field over which moral responsibility must be exercised. The manager must not go too far. The organization's extension of paternal authority and its demand for a special allegiance

'is socially irresponsible usurpation, indefensible on the grounds alike of public policy and the enterprise's self interest. The company is not and must never claim to be home, family, religion, life or fate for the individual. It must never interfere in his private life or his citizenship. He is tied to the company through a voluntary and cancellable employment contract, not through some mystical and indissoluble bond.'

(Drucker 1968: 461)

That is a sensible and practical limitation of the power of over-mighty subjects for which we might all have cause to be grateful, but it does beg several questions. Drucker escapes from them through the familiar obscurities of pluralism: management is *a* leading group but not *the* leading group; it must be held in place by the state, the law, and other social institutions. Economic institutions are powerful but they must not become over-weening: 'if the enterprise ever forgets this, society will retaliate by making its own supreme institution, the state, omnipotent' (Drucker 1968: 460). The ethics of management and its social responsibility are therefore limited to what immediately concerns its own (economic) interest and then to what impact it must inevitably have upon society in general. But at this wider level of concern, responsibility remains limited to an awareness of what society can do to business, which must not be bothered about what business can do to society. Indeed, if business goes too far, society will threaten it by legislative and political control. The ethics of management are instrumentally directed to the support of the economic direction of business affairs; managers' concern with ethics derives from the pursuit of their own and their organization's economic goals.

There are two objections to this view, objections that need to be pressed despite the liberal and humane gloss with which it is presented. The first is that it is a view of moral responsibility that takes it out of the field of ethics. It is, at the least, a naïve view of moral responsibility that confines the consequences of my actions to my own self-interest and excludes any real concern with consequences for others. Other people, other groups, agencies, states, society itself, exist in moral terms only in so far as they may threaten me, and my care for them must be confined to causing them the least disturbance lest they should disturb me. It is also a singularly material view of ethics. It would once have been entirely acceptable to official Marxist doctrine in which moral feelings and judgements were explained as the disguised emanations of material and economic class interests; objective moral judgements were impossible, they merely represented the self-interested perspective of a class pressing its own advantage. Marxists have, for the most part, abandoned that position as too crude and the current tendency among them is to stress the genuinely moral aspects of Marx's theory. Suffice it to suggest here that management's conception of its own ethical concern seems to fit perfectly the severest and most sceptical account that Marxists have ever given of it.

The second objection takes us back to the view of management as an economic organ, the 'specifically economic organ of an industrial society' and therefore reflecting the 'basic spirit of the modern age'. This is by no means an eccentric view of how managerial, bureaucratic organizations have been seen as industrialization has developed. It goes back to the pre-eminence ascribed by Saint-Simon to the new group of 'industrials', to

Weber's account of the domination of bureaucratic control directed at the achievement of economic goals, to Marx's analysis of the power of capitalism's drive for profit (and his prediction that the drive would be self-defeating), to Durkheim's attempt to derive moral relationships from the only conceivable basis in modern society, the network of business relationships and the division of labour. All sides conspire in agreement as to the economic foundation of the 'basic spirit of the modern age'. The only significant disagreement is about the role of management. The argument descending from Burnham and from Berle and Means, that there is a managerial revolution or, at least, that there has been a significant split between management and business ownership, is merely a schism within a prevailing orthodoxy in which one side says that managers have emerged as a distinct group, more rational and more authoritative than the owners who hired them, while the others insist that there has been no change, managers are merely the puppets of their capitalist masters. But no one doubts their centrality to the basic spirit of the modern age.

The point was made by MacIntyre but he derives a different conclusion from the same premiss. He accepts the whole weight of sociological authority that the manager is one of the 'central characters' of the modern age but he sees no ground for arguing from reality that the manager must be, or can become, the agent of moral repair. Why should he? There is no logical connection between a fact and a moral conclusion from it; what is does not necessarily entail what should be. MacIntyre argues that the pre-eminence of the manager has contributed to moral decay, to the breakdown of the possibility of moral relationships and moral discourse. Managers' claim to effectiveness (the 'specific problem' as I have just labelled it), while in itself specious, is 'inseparable from a mode of human existence in which the contrivance of means is in central part the manipulation of human beings into compliant patterns of behaviour' (MacIntyre 1981: 71). Lest we think he exaggerates, let us turn to that most humane agency of management, the Institute of Personnel Management.

'It is probable that the majority of managers now at work will never receive another promotion. There are several forces at work in society which suggest that managers and professional staff will reach their career plateau earlier in their working lives than was customary in the past. For a previous generation of managers, the expectations of career advancement provided the main motivational spur. If that expectation is no longer perceived then there are important implications for the morale and motivation of a large group of men and women whose loyalty and enthusiasm are essential for the well being of all organisations.'

(IPM 1985: 6)

The 'important implications' for the organization suggest that managers cannot be seen as an homogeneous group because some of them have to be managed or manipulated by others. (For a discussion of the way in which management is likely to turn upon itself in this respect see my *The Ideology of Work*, chapter 14.)

Or, put more simply: if managers' loyalty depends upon career advancement, how else is loyalty to be maintained without it? We can avoid all imputations of cynicism while still suggesting that this seems to amount to a search for means for the manipulation of human beings into compliant patterns of behaviour.

It must be acknowledged that the seriousness of the charge laid against management by MacIntyre is no ground for rejecting it. But the problem he raises is so severe and its consequence so pessimistic that we must search for a solution. Let us begin by suggesting, in due humility, that Professor MacIntyre's argument is more convincing than his understanding of management. If there is error here it is not his fault, he has gone to the best authorities and brought from them a received view of what managers are and what they do. I am going to suggest that, if his account of management is correct, then his gloomy conclusions must be accepted, but that his account may be mistaken. If that is the case then we have at least the possibility of escape from those conclusions.

Two principal accounts of management are available; we shall call the first official theory, the second real theory.

Official theory is the classic account of management as rational, purposive activity directed at the efficient achievement of goals usually determined in economic terms. Official theory descends from administrative science and incorporates a number of fields. It rests upon the sub-division of work according to the requirements of efficient production engineering, the reduction of discretionary judgement in the subordinate worker, the standardization and control of movements, and the operation of a pre-determined and closely planned task. Work study and the close analysis and re-design of jobs are intended to reduce errors and cost, to maximize the control exercised by the task over the worker and to minimize time wasted in unnecessary operations and movements. Training is a necessary accompaniment to this process of analysis because it requires that task routines should be acquired quickly and without individual deviations. At the same time, the whole production process is broken down into a systematic sequence so that raw materials, tools, and labour can be deployed in the most effective manner. Thus individual movements, tasks, and jobs, together with the production process as a whole, are all determined according to a pre-conceived plan so as to provide order, predictability, and control.

Ideally, the process is self-controlling, subjected to Follett's 'law of the situation' and requiring Taylor's 'democratic' submission to it of everyone involved in its function, including managers. Henry Ford thus derives his axiom that 'work and the work alone control us' in two senses: that we are all subordinated to its economic ends and that we are subjected to the logical requirements of its detailed planning. In practice, supervision and control contrive to be necessary to deal with unexpected contingencies (changes in raw material quality, machine breakdown, and human 'error' – the incorrigible tendency of workers to be human).

The organization of 'line' control is comparatively simple, subject, once upon a time to basic tenets concerning the maximum 'span of control' that one individual could effectively exercise over others. Complex production processes also require the co-ordination of specialized activities like the allocation of costs to processes, the maintenance of equipment, the provision of inspection and quality control, the purchase of supplies, the marketing, merchandizing, and distribution of the product, and, in a final irony, the management of the 'personnel', the

supervision of which begins to break away from its subordination to the task. All these activities are grouped together
according to function and they require a proliferating organization of increasing complexity. The design of the organization
itself becomes a matter of special concern and reason for a belief
that 'Some universally optimum structure of formal managerial
roles and procedures was attainable through systematic study'
(Child 1969: 85). Such simple faith in 'the one best way' has
now been abandoned in favour of a more sophisticated
acknowledgment that organization is influenced by technology,
market, its own history, and even 'culture'; simple and standard
organization charts have been replaced by the arcane activities
of Organizational Design consultants. Latterly, official theory
has taken account of the advice of behavioural scientists who
have discovered that human individuals and groups bring their
own problems and potentials that effective organizations might
be advised to take into account in their plans.

In whatever way it develops, official theory sees managers
acting rationally within purposive organizations. Some of the
phenomena that they have to account for include non-rational
subordinate human inhabitants of organizations having a
regrettable tendency to be influenced, on occasions, by their
emotions rather than their reason – but understanding aided by
research can incorporate such deviance. The 'scientific' claims
of official theory are, of course, the target for the first of
MacIntyre's criticisms, that management's claim to arrive at
law-like generalizations is false. Even so, the claim carries its
own utility if it is advanced with sufficient persuasion because
it becomes the basis (however shaky) for the exercise of moral
authority, the script for management's histrionic performance.
Official management theory is useful even if its pretensions to
science are unmasked as irrelevant to improved performance.
Thus, Astley suggests that

'management theory is not predominantly oriented toward
achieving higher levels of organisational performance. . . .
Management theorists are engaged in the provision of a
cosmology within which managers can locate their missions
and actions as meaningful. In this regard management
theorists affect managers not so much at a practical level . . .

but at an ideational level, in terms of managers' attribution of meaning and significance to these practical actions. Theory achieves this by making symbolic sense of, and imputing subjective meaning to managers' practical experiences. It locates those experiences within an overarching cosmology. This cosmology is shrouded in a "scientific" guise, but management science is important largely for its symbolic function.'

(Astley 1984: 18)

What official theory seems to provide, then, is some basis for persuading others that managers know what they are about, and some comfort for the managers in maintaining the illusion with the necessary confidence. In either case, official theory does not seem to be very real. More and more evidence has accumulated ever since the Hawthorn experiments that a great deal of the behaviour of the subordinates in organizations cannot be understood by attempting to enclose it in a theory of rational, goal-directed activity subsumed under the organization's grand design and purpose. More recently, the foreman and supervisors, once seen as the front line of management, came to be described as 'the lost managers', also excluded from the formal organization in that their behaviour cannot be comprehended in rational, goal-directed terms (Child and Partridge 1982). Official theory is driven to come to terms, if it can, with a culture of work and norms of behaviour that resist and react to the formal organization's attempts to control it. Official theory's view of managerial organization is seriously dented.

Real theory provides a different account. Dalton listed the collusions and contradictions that interfered with the organization's direct achievement of its goals. They included the inability of superordinates to learn from their subordinates about what was going on, the self-protective feigning of ignorance, the side-stepping of official procedures to gain personal advantage, the deliberate use of change and confusion, the resort to simple expediency in the face of excessive formal demands, the construction and maintenance of deliberately ambiguous rules, and the claims and obligations of friendship (Dalton 1959: 52). He concluded that bureaucratic theory (what I have called official theory) 'slights the fact that in the larger organisations, local and personal demands take precedence in most cases' and that 'the typical firm is thus a shifting set of contained disruption, powered and guided by differentially skilled and committed persons. Its unofficial aspects bulk large but are shrouded in a bureaucratic cloak' (Dalton 1959:265, 270). Evidence has accumulated further to support this kind of view. Managers spend most of their time, up to 90 per cent of it, talking (Steward 1982), and most of their conversations are brief, desultory, and unscheduled, uncontained by the order of any organization chart. Effective managers build and maintain wide personal networks extending to subordinates, the subordinates of other managers, members of other departments, and members of other organizations. They construct their own priorities and agendas, have their own ways of acquiring and distributing resources, and they frequently regard the formal controls and channels of the organization as irrelevant (Kotter 1982). Research in hospital organizations suggests that such conclusions cannot be confined to the most successful of general managers. Ward Sisters and Nursing Officers use the formal system and its allocation to them of formal authority only in unusual circumstances of the breakdown when their own ability to call upon obligations, friendships, the general commitment to patient care, quite independently of any formal divisions of the organization, occasionally turns out to be inadequate. The general conclusion from what I have termed real theory is that a great deal of the behaviour in managerial organizations is social and political in character.

The point of this distinction between official and real theory is to suggest that if MacIntyre's criticism of management is confined to the official view of its activity, and if that view is mistaken, then management may be innocent of the charge of moral corruption. We shall also need to return to the distinction he makes between 'practice' and 'institution' (MacIntyre 1981: 125). A practice is a social and co-operative human activity realizing goods that are internal but determined by human conceptions of excellence and value. Internal goods are judged by those inside the practice but their achievement is a good for the whole community. Institutions are more likely to be concerned with the production of external goods in a competitive exchange with winners and losers. Practices require and depend upon institutions to carry them forward, but they are also threatened by their competitiveness and corrupted by the external goods with which they are concerned. Architecture, farming, and teaching are practices. Management is, or it inhabits, institutions, engaged in distributive competition and devoid of virtue. To the extent that practices require institutions they have to be managed and to that extent they are corrupted, their only defence their concern with internal goods sustained by virtue.

There is more to it than that, however. The traditional professions, we can take it, are practices (many of them, including medicine, actually employ the term in common usage). They are sustained by self-governing institutions like the British Medical Association, the Royal College of Surgeons, the Law Society, the Inns of Court. Because of their specialist knowledge and their concern with public and important goods (health and justice) society deems it necessary for them to regulate their own affairs and that recognition is acknowledged in law and by charter. But the institutions that have to be established to administer these practices can become, if not corrupt, overly concerned with the protection of their professional inhabitants. The maintenance of standards of practice is rightly related to the examination of competence and knowledge and thence to the restriction of entry to the profession to those who have qualified. But the control of a labour market is an effective way of monopolizing it and of maintaining the income and status of those who dominate it. C. Wright Mills, describing the extent to which the American medical profession had succumbed to the 'managerial demiurge' wrote that

> 'the profession as a whole is politically uninterested or ignorant; its members are easy victims and ready exponents of the U.S. businessman's psychology of individualism, in which liberty means no state interference, except a rigid state licensing system. The professional ethics in which this interest group clothes its business drive is an obsolete mythology, but it has been of great use to those who would adapt themselves to predatory ways.'
>
> (Mills 1956: 119–20)

Professional practices, Wright Mills would say, turn themselves into bureaucratic institutions, succumbing to a competitive scramble for external goods and becoming almost devoid of virtue. But the professions are never entirely and in sole charge of their own affairs and of the 'goods' that should be their concern. They are licensed and protected by statutory regulation, and legislation (with whatever necessary reservations we care to make) is broadly representative of the community's needs and expectations. Practices, says MacIntyre, are concerned with goods internal to those practices, with standards of excellence that are determined by human conceptions of what is good for the whole community. The conception of a 'good', though its realization may be regulated by professional institutions, is determined and defined by a community. If the institution breaks away from that conception and its general definition, if it loses the trust of the community in its virtue, then it is heading for trouble. The growing incidence of the prosecution of doctors for damages arising from incompetence (pioneered in the USA incidentally and proliferating in Britain), the weakening of the control exercised by solicitors over the conveyancing of property, and the freeing of the provision of spectacles from the control of opticians are instances of just that sort of trouble.

The problem goes further, perhaps, than MacIntyre would take it. Institutions, certainly, cannot be trusted to regulate their affairs in the public interest. Any institutional arrangement for the maintenance of 'goods', the preservation of standards of conduct and codes of ethics, is likely to be unreliable and may tend towards self-interested corruption. Practices, because they are carried forward by institutions are for that reason unreliable and similarly untrustworthy. It would seem that no good can come out of either.

Such would be the case if we saw them as detached from their social setting and isolated from the public view. Practices and institutions are different things and the relationship between them is symbiotic, but they do not simply relate to each other and they are not immune from other influences. Practices realize and are concerned with goods as they are defined by the community, with human conceptions of excellence and value. Practices may then mediate between 'socially established cooperative human activity' and the institutions' requirement to fulfil different functions and meet different and necessary needs. While institutions tend to the corruption of practices they also further their purpose by contributing energy and efficiency to their pursuit. It may be that the tendency to corruption is held in check, to some extent, by the contrary demand from the community of the practices upon which it depends for its survival. The institutions themselves, necessary to the survival of practices, are not isolated from the influence of the community because they are staffed and maintained by its citizens. We have observed that even the most competitive of commercial institutions is aware of at least a defensive concern for public opinion and the law and is likely to show a self-interested degree of responsibility in its activities. That may not be sufficient to conclude that institutions are essentially moral in the way that they construct their affairs, but it may be as much as we can expect from them and it is something of significance.

This is to suggest that the community is not without influence, first upon the definition of goods that practices provide, and second upon the character and behaviour of the institutions that maintain them. All is not necessarily lost. But we may concede that institutions and their internal arrange-ments are not to be trusted as safeguards of the public good or for the realization of 'goods'. Nor are institutional arrangements and procedures to be trusted for the maintenance of ethical safeguards and the preservation of goods for that is not their purpose.

The real distinction between 'practice' and 'institution' is none too clear. We know roughly what we mean by 'institution' or 'organization' allowing, that is, for a degree of reification (who has ever seen an organization?). Institutions or organiz-ations at least occupy buildings with front doors. Practices, how-ever, are more diffuse and abstract, more difficult to conceive of unless they are related to activities engaged in by people in places. Medicine, the law, teaching, farming; where do they take place other than in hospitals, courts, schools, and farms? Practices not only require institutions to carry them forward, they inhabit them and are, to the common view, indistinguish-able from them. 'Practice' and 'institution' are often two aspects of the same thing. If the practice of teaching is carried on in schools is it not conceivable that the practice of management is carried on in business or service organizations? We are correctly reminded that they are different kinds of concern with different preoccupations and values often held in contra-distinction to each other, but this is simply to suggest that there is a dialectic of forces at work in such activities and that, in one or the other case, or at different times, the one force may be stronger than the other, as C. Wright Mills argued of the American medical profession.

The question is whether management or the bureaucratic process can be seen as the characteristic activity of institutions opposed, hip and thigh, to the practices that exhibit ethical concern. My attempted exposure of the banality of the case for 'business ethics' would suggest that it is a real distinction, that MacIntyre is right, that managerial institutions are the death incarnate of the moral concern exhibited by practices. But it is possible that the attack might have been more properly directed against the 'official theory' of management and, if we have succeeded in suggesting that official theory is a false account, then it is possible that the attack is spent upon a mistaken target.

The problem is not as unreal (or as 'academic', as the word is synonymously used: what does that elision imply of the practice of university teaching and of what the community makes of it?) as my treatment of it might so far have suggested. We are concerned with authority, with management's authority, and I have argued (in chapter 6) that authority must have a moral foundation, that it cannot be assured by the obfuscations of employment policies, however liberally disguised, and that it is finally likely to rest upon a degree of public consensus as to the goods that management produces, upon, when the batteries of instrumental techniques are set aside, what management is understood to be for.

Now it is conceivable (no more than that can be claimed), if the distinction between official and real theory is a proper one and if the malodorous consequences of management's behaviour are confined to the former which is deemed to be mistaken, that something can be rescued from what real theory makes of management. It is conceivable that a practice of management, comparable with the practice of medicine, teaching, or law, can be discerned as emerging from real theory. If that is the case, it is possible that a moral foundation, far from being destroyed by management (in its official version), may be derived from real managerial behaviour. If a practice of management can be constructed on the foundation of what managers do rather than upon an ideological account of what they do, then it might be possible to construct a moral foundation for management and that, in turn, could establish a foundation for managerial authority.

One of the most distinctive features of accounts of managerial behaviour in real theory concerns its social and political character. Kotter observed that if 'professional' management depended upon 'formal techniques and structures in a well-organised, practical, and reflective way, then none of these managers behaved very professionally' (Kotter 1982: 8). Successful general managers created agendas and networks that were consistent with but different from the formal versions, they developed networks of co-operative relationships using a wide variety of face-to-face methods: 'They tried to make others feel legitimately obliged to them by doing favours. . . . They acted in ways to encourage others to identify with this' (1982: 69). Further, general managers achieved much of their influence 'by using symbolic methods. That is they used meetings, architecture, language, stories about the organisation, time and space as symbols in order to communicate messages indirectly' (1982: 74). As long ago as 1959, Dalton had observed that bureaucratic theory 'slights the fact that in the larger organisation, local and personal demands take precedence in most cases' and that within a degree of general conformity to the formal organization of the business 'many individual managers and workers do "fight" the organisation' and that individual dynamics, deliberate misinterpretations, interests, and alliances are very important (Dalton 1959: 265). More recently Rosemary Stewart has re-emphasized that 'the traditional picture of managerial work . . . of rationality, planning and pursuit of organisational goals' (in Earl 1983: 82), is in part misleading, that management is a political activity, that 'managers may not necessarily pursue the interests of the organisation, or formal organisational goals' (in Earl 1983: 91). Burns, in an account of hospital organization, distinguishes between the collaborative system and the managerial system. The former is not akin to sets of institutional rules and specific routines but is under-written by rules of practice (his very word, as it happens) concerning training, negotiation, and trust: 'managerialism is grounded in distrust in much the same way as the collaborative system is grounded in trust' (Burns 1981: 9). He concludes that the real work is done through informal meetings and arrange-ments and 'that the real strength of the organisation lies in the collaborative system' (1981: 13), that the standard view of the organization is that it is 'rationally ordered according to coherent and unitary principles. It is no such thing' (1981: 30). In a recent and monumental study of ICI, Pettigrew observed that theories of organization choice and change have greatest value if they incorporate a political and cultural analysis of organizational life.

'The recognition that organisational culture can shape and not merely reflect organisational power relationships directs attention both to the ground rules which structure the character of the political process inside the firms, and the assumption and interests which powerful groups shield and lower groups may only with fortitude challenge. The acts and processes associated with politics as the management of meaning represent conceptually the overlap between a concern with the political and cultural analyses of organis-ations. A central concept linking political and cultural analyses particularly germane to the understanding of con-tinuity and change is legitimacy. The management of meaning refers to a process of symbol construction and value designed to create legitimacy for one's ideas, actions and demands, and to delegitimise the demands of one's opponents. Key concepts for analysing these processes of legitimisation are symbolism, language, ideology and myth.'

(Pettigrew 1985: 442)

We have already observed, in the distinction drawn between real theory and official theory, that the latter's emphasis on bureaucratic rationality is both exaggerated (or unreal) and that its utility can be explained in ideological terms, deemed necessary to the maintenance of managerial authority. We have also suggested that the ideological defence of that authority, while it rests on an unconvincing presumption of science, is spurious. Subordinate workers do not believe it, managers do not believe it, and MacIntyre's unmasking leaves it with few shreds of respectability. It survives in the business school curricula, perhaps, as the intellectual accompaniment to that process of insulation that is characteristic of the practical programme of employment policies consistently pursued by British managers.

The conclusion that emerges consistently from recent and authoritative accounts of the real activity of managers is that, because they are concerned with social and political relationships in organizations, they have a real concern with moral relationships. Let us return to an earlier study of the BBC, by Tom Burns, to make the point explicitly. The people at the top of that organization, as of any other, he said, see it as a large, ordered collectivity directed at the achievement of their goals and 'infused with a moral order of its own'. He pointed out that

> 'these feelings are real enough, but only in a particular sense. Read as a consensus, or a common ethos, it is usually spurious – if regarded as applying to the organisational hierarchy. If, however, the object of such feelings is seen as a community – a working community – a specific, limited but important significance attaches to them.'
>
> (Burns 1977: 84)

He refers to the work of Robert Park, of E. P. Thompson, and of N. E. Lang to demonstrate that organizations consist of a network of games in which individuals have the double role of players and spectators and that the whole is held together by a moral order. He explains that

> 'when one speaks of a moral order prevailing in a working community as large as the B.B.C., what is under discussion is not some pervasive social conscience which is absorbed by recruits through some process of ethical osmosis but part of the actualities of the talks and actions which constitute work.'
>
> (Burns 1977: 84)

The paradox of this conclusion is that we are left with the conviction that the unofficial network is more of a moral order than the official hierarchy that seeks to impose moral duty upon its subordinates. The means by which this moral order is attained are strange, at least to the language of bureaucracy. Burns speaks of games, Pettigrew of language and myth, Kotter of symbolic methods, symbols, and stories about the organization. Such language may be strange to management theory (although recently imported: see for example Michael Thomas's 'In Search of Culture' in *Personnel Management*, September, 1985; the fact that the language has been distorted and the point missed, as in all importations to management 'theory', is revealed by Mr Thomas's sub-title: 'Holy Grail or Gravy Train'). It is not strange in sociology and anthropology. We may recall Gouldner's emphasis on the importance of norms of reciprocity, the sense of obligation and expectation that bound individuals to each other in the community to which they belonged. His study of a gypsum mine emphasized the importance of a negotiated order in the network of work relationships and the consequence of its disturbance (Gouldner 1955).

The connection between moral order and the community has been still more closely observed in anthropological studies. Redfield suggested that the scientific atomization and analysis of the parts and activities of a community missed the point, that models of machines or organisms might not be appropriate and that a more real and total understanding might be achieved by 'using words and thoughts that do not readily find acceptance in the natural sciences but rather are appropriate to drama or other forms of literary art' (Redfield 1960: 16). He speculated that it might be possible to write a 'generalised biography' about a little community in which one would describe the 'technology not as an organised system of operations in which men, women and children take part' (1960: 56–7) and that

'it might be possible to say something about the hastening of a little community from the inside view. Such a history would be a people's own story as that people have come to conceive it. It would show how a group conceives its unity in relation to time.'

(Redfield 1960: 110)

The intimacy between work in organizations and communities and the language of 'drama and other forms of literary art' can be seen in the study of narrative. Barbara Hardy, giving an account of the stories told in *The Rainbow*, the inn in George Eliot's *Silas Marner*, tells us that the principal storyteller has to be given cues and that the stories that follow are familiar, falling into an expected rhythm, forming a well-observed ritual. 'The scene in *The Rainbow* is not just cleverly contrived entertainment but a self-analysing drama of the community. . . . The drama consists of telling and listening to stories which are a part of the history of the parish' (Hardy 1975: 135). But Silas Marner has been excluded from membership of this community:

> 'Silas's story-telling takes a first step towards that social restoration which is the subject of the novel, and the society into which he steps is that of the communal story, those annals of the parish to which he will belong. *The Rainbow* decides that Silas is not a ghost and takes him into the company, which has been impressively and soberly established through the story-telling, making him free of its ease and its humanity.'
>
> (Hardy 1975: 135)

The conclusions that begin to emerge from this diffuse discussion are that managerial organizations, at least in real theory accounts of their inhabitants' behaviour, can be seen as communities; that they are held together by informal moral relationships that may be stronger than the moral order that the hierarchical superstructures seek to impose, and that moral and social relationships are cemented by myth, symbol, culture, and narrative. I suggest that this interpretation squares with experience, with the every-day story of management folk. Quite apart from the evidence presented by real theorists as to the importance of stories (Kotter tells us that in several encounters the general managers regarded the substantive issues as a waste of time while the discussions 'typically contained a considerable amount of joking, kidding, and non-work related issues. The humour was often about others in the organisation or industry' (Kotter 1982: 80)), any one who has worked in a managerial organization will confirm the importance of stories. When the store is closed, the office shut, or the day shift gone home, the senior cadre gathers in the 'old man's' office or they repair for the happy hour. The ritual may look like an extension of work and evidence of total commitment to the company but what actually happens is that the inchoate events of the day are given structure and meaning in stories from which, like Silas Marner, the more junior managers are excluded. The daily cycle of events given narrative form are overtaken by the stories told at the annual conferences, usually about last year's conference and the mythical activities of heroes (in one field of endeavour or another), and the best of them accrete with a general story of the firm, its past, its great men, its triumphs and disasters overcome. That story *is* the organization, which newcomers must learn like new recruits to a regiment. A great deal of the reality of organizations, as distinct from reified conceptualization, as it is perceived by their inhabitants, takes narrative form. What it is like to work for Ford, what Ford is, is narrative.

Managerial organizations share this characteristic of narrative understanding with communities because they *are* communities. If this is true then we find that one of the gravest charges against them, that the most effective bureaucrat (or manager) is the best actor, loses its critical tone: if storytelling or histrionic success is what gives success in our culture, and if storytelling is the *real* activity of managers, then it is what they do, their significant activity, rather than a disguise for some sinister and covert plot. Narrative is, after all, MacIntyre tells us, a proper and important process. The maintenance of a community depends upon tradition, a living tradition emerges from the past, from history, and it is conducted in a narrative. And, he goes on, the creation and maintenance of communities is a practice realizing goods concerned with standards of excellence determined by human conceptions of ends that are valued. But if this is the case management too, like teaching, and architecture, and farming, may be or might become a practice. If the characterization of the best manager as the best actor or best narrator actually fits real theory's accounts of managerial activity then it is not so much an indictment as an accurate description and one that contains the possibility of virtue rather than vice.

The attack on management as the institutional enemy of practices, the claimant to authority based upon pseudo-science and false theory, the hypocritical destroyer of moral discourse, is an attack directed at the ideological posture that management has adopted or has been persuaded to adopt by its educators.

Real accounts suggest that the attack is misdirected at a disguise that is ineffective.

There are two problems to be encountered before this transformation of management from villain to hero, from the subvertor of civilization to its rescuer, is accomplished. The metamorphosis has been made to depend upon management's role as defender of a community, but with which community is management identifiable? The choice is wide. Any community, so-called, is fissured in a variety of ways, by reference to class, income, education, economic interest, kinship, locality, age, access to power, religious affiliation, political outlook, or occupation. The problems of identifying a community in complex societies encouraged earlier anthropologists to examine the simplest forms in order to reduce such variables as far as possible. The problem of identification is always there, however, but it does not prevent our speaking of the community in a sensible way, even in the most complex societies. I have, in any case, side-stepped the problems to some extent by arguing that the authority of management will derive from the community's approval for what management does, for its ends. That is no more loose than, and just as meaningful a suggestion as, the ordinary and unavoidable usage by which we speak of the community's concern for the elderly, for the sick, for the reduction of crime, or for measures to be taken in its own defence. Government and opposition, and the measure of agreement between them, are largely dependent upon a meaningful if uncertain and debatable conception of what the community is and how its most general interests are to be met. It is likely, indeed, that without a working idea of a community, government is impossible. In that most vague and general of senses, I have suggested that management has (or should have) a relationship to the community at large. But this is a very general analogy, reliable only in the broadest sense and likely to seem unreliable on any close examination because, although a responsibility to the community in general is conceivable, there is no close parallel between the role of government and of management.

Management's position is more particular and more complex. Management stands in a special relationship to the enterprise, public or privately owned, in the latter case to its shareholders and board of directors. The organization and its owners can thus be seen as the community that management has a special duty to foster. There would be no problem about deriving managerial practice and its attendant moral responsibility from a community in this sense. Many ICI managers spoke of the company as 'a great ship ploughing through waters and not needing to change' (Pettigrew 1985: 387) and we do not need to be informed by the current interest in organizational 'culture' to know that most managers identify themselves with their company, within limits and respecting qualifications proper to the extent that anyone identifies with any community. Managers, like the rest of us, will look after themselves, may even have occupational or professional interests that cut across company boundaries, and will, like the rest of us, own to a variety of other loyalties and affiliations, but they remain, to some extent, company men. That extent is at least a measure of this enclosure in a meaningful community with whose interest and survival they will identify.

Meaningful it may be but it must be acknowledged that the organizational community is fissured and friable. To what extent does it enclose all its members? The extent to which management is at pains to press or persuade its subordinate employees into a sense of committed membership suggests that there is a perceived problem of differentiated affiliation. There must be question as to how far subordinate labour is alienated from the organization as a community. It is doubtful whether this question can be answered at all sensibly at an empirical level but there is little doubt that the distinction between committed or contained management and alienated or excluded labour is exaggerated by the official view that organization takes of itself. The economic rationale that encloses an organization misinterprets the real activity of its managers and requires the interpretation of subordinate labour's behaviour as deviant or alienated. It is not so much that labour is excluded from the organizational community as that the theory of organization cannot realistically comprehend labour within it: it is the theory that is occluded rather than the labour that is essentially excluded. The epistemological problem is exacerbated by the behaviour to which it gives rise. A theory of organization as community would not only illuminate the actually co-operative activity that suffuses all members of an enterprise (if it did not, no enterprise would hold together for very long); it would also remove the artificial barriers to understanding that discourage the development of co-operation.

> 'The traditional division into two sides may not appear to be so realistic if one of the sides is not so committed to the values which it has been understood to impose, unsuccessfully, upon the other. If both are . . . enclosed in a community, then the theoretical relationships between them may begin to appear as a practical managerial responsibility instead of a futile attempt to bridge the chasm of alienation.'
> (Gustavsson, Karlsson, and Räftegård 1985: 119)

The argument that the exclusion of the proletariat from the enterprise is exaggerated by official theory and can be reduced by that theory's amendment is none too different from the behavioural scientist's appeal that organizations should be re-shaped in human terms in order to reduce cognitive dissonance and the human subordinate's self-preserving necessity to fight for his human corner within them. But how far is it realistic to regard the business organization as essentially human?

This is the most difficult question to be directed against a real theory account of business enterprise. Once again we are faced with a formidable alliance between Marxist and Manchester School economists who concur, if in nothing else, in the explanation that business organization is directed solely at the maximization of profit and that, from that end, a series of rational steps follow that entail, *inter alia*, the treatment of labour as a resource or means. The weakness of this imposing consensus lies precisely in the universality and simplicity of its judgement. The end and purpose of all business organizations is certainly the attainment of economic aims; if they are not achieved the business cannot survive. All organizations are similarly constrained. Universities, monasteries, and hospitals are all ultimately concerned with the achievement of economic ends; so are rugby clubs (league and union) and charities. Mr Micawber reminded us of the same ultimate truth in his homily on domestic income and expenditure. The economic explanation of the purpose of business organization and the paramount importance it ascribes to profit is a universal truth, which therefore explains very little. It further fails to make any effective distinctions between the long-term and necessary goals of the organization and the short-term and intermediate practical goals of its inhabitants. There is no necessary and imminent connection between the organization's ultimate need to receive a surplus of income over expenditure and the day-to-day motivation of its inhabitants. In the long run we are all dead, but that unavoidable conclusion does not significantly influence the way that most of us live.

If the inhabitants of organizations have, to say the least, considerable leeway in the decisions they take and in the way they behave before they reach the ultimate influence of economic necessity, then there is much to explain short of a crude and simple economic determinism. Part of that explanation can surely contain a view of the organization and its inhabitants as a community. If it is acceptable, then it releases the potential for understanding managers as representatives and leaders of that community. The potential itself may be sufficient reason for advocating a community theory of organizational management but that would be hortatory and, while not improper, is to be postponed. For the nonce it is sufficient to say that to explain organizations as communities and managers as engaged in their social and political maintenance is conceivable, that it fits actual accounts of behaviour as well as, or better than, the formalized abstractions of bureaucratic rationality which actually seem to explain very little.

The economic purpose of business organizations is certainly one of the explanations of the belief that their managers occupy one of the central roles of our age. It is not, as Adam Smith reminded us, out of regard for our welfare that the baker bakes our bread or the brewer brews our beer – it is their economic interest that assures our breakfast and our evening solace. But breweries and bakeries do not continue in the complexity of their daily operations out of a close calculation of the economic interest of each of their employees, nor by reference to a contracted or coercive control of the activities of each of their subordinates. They survive as managed communities and the other important explanation of the manager as a central character of our age has to be found in the importance of his role in relation to the community both little (his organization) and at large. It is the failure to comprehend or accept that communal role (a failure encouraged by the myopic perception of the economic as exclusively important) that has concerned a tradition of social criticism that relates Durkheim and Elton Mayo, both insisting that the social and moral problem of industrial control must become a central concern in an industrial society. More recently, Dahrendorf has argued that 'the notion of a capitalist society is an extrapolation from economic to social relations' (1959: 37), that it assumes some formative power on the part of economic structures, and that the assumption is singularly weak. Some 150 years earlier that prototype management consultant Andrew Ure observed, in *The Philosophy of Manufacturers*, that economic theory fails to motivate anyone and he recommended employers to attend to the construction of the moral machinery of their factories with as much concern as they attended to its engineering.

I have suggested that no serious attempt has ever been made or, at least, that such efforts that have been launched at achieving the commitment of employees have been so patently cynical, or have been so bedevilled by insulating policies of employment designed to release management from any moral concern for its subordinates, as to be still-born. In that sense British management deserves the severest of criticism directed at it from the exposure of its moral and intellectual poverty by Fox and MacIntyre, together with a range of radical critics. But the real targets of such criticism, it would seem, are the educators of management, who have successively misunderstood and misrepresented its real purpose and activity.

If managers are to be encouraged to see themselves as maintainers of social and political networks of co-operation engaged in the practice of community maintenance they must see themselves as exercising power. If that power is to be perceived by the members of the communities they govern as authoritatively exercised, conceived to be legitimate, then managers must be taught both that their influence is real and that its exercise requires moral as well as practical significance. The question that next arises is whether they will be encouraged by this extension of their perception of their own role to be even more manipulative and covert in their machinations than they have already been accused of being. Are we simply proposing that managers should be prepared to occupy the position of the ruling élite that Burnham predicted for them in *The Managerial Revolution* (1942)?

It may be that we are. No account, right, left, or centre, fails to conclude that managers are one of the 'central characters of our time', influential over the lives of others, far-reaching in the decisions they take, casting in hegemonic mould the way that we think of the purpose and policies of manufacturing industry, retail, health care, broadcasting, education, and welfare. Whether the manager in his histrionic performance is conceived of as villain or as hero, no one concludes that he has a minor part in the contemporary drama. The advice as to what we should do with his part takes one of three forms. The standard consultancy view is that his performance should be improved by better technique and improved make-up and lighting so that he can become a more convincing play-actor and, hence, more properly the victim of MacIntyre's searching criticism. This advice pays little or no regard to the social setting in which the manager's role is played out, apart from a cursory defence of capitalism, unchanged in its tone and content since the vulgarizations of nineteenth-century *laissez-faire* economics and, whatever its reliability as economic theory, irrelevant and unmoving in its appeal for moral commitment. The second re-casting of the manager's role requires that, before his performance can be credible and his authority legitimate, the entire social and economic environment in which he performs must be changed; it is not his part but the drama that must alter. For the communist the manager is a villain, the agent of the capitalist in exploiting the proletariat whether as a worker or consumer. We should remember in passing, however, that recent Marxist studies are more perceptive in their analysis and explanation of the ways in which the manager seeks to achieve the co-operation of labour than are much of management or consultancy advice: a reading in radical labour process theory is often a better grounding in labour management than a text in personnel management. That reservation aside, radical critics cannot concede legitimate authority to management unless it plays its part in a communist drama. The third re-casting comes from the counter-culture and would seem to abominate the managerial role even more thoroughly. The technocracy, which breeds and supports management in the control of large organizations and mass-production and mass-consumption, is condemned in terms of its dis-utility, its wastefulness of natural resources, its production of 'illth' rather than wealth (Ruskin's term), and the damage that it does to its human employees and customers. The counter-culture sees managers as the creatures of large-scale industry, converging, whether privately or publicly owned, upon a joint course to disaster. The critics of the technocracy, such as Roszak or Illich seem anxious not merely to change the role, or even the play, in which managers act: they wish to tear down the theatre or, at least, that it be destroyed by natural catastrophe.

The reader, particularly if he is a manager, might properly ask at this point what conceivable role can be recommended for management's performance in this embracing and condemnatory criticism. What *can* it do with at least some hope for the suspension of disbelief?

I am proposing that, within the existing economic framework, we should recognize the existence of what Arthur Giddens (1979) calls 'levels of structuration'. Giddens has argued, in a succession of impressive attacks upon the traditional pre-conceptions of both functionalist and Marxist sociology, that, within a system of social relationships that exert powerful constraints upon human responses, the capacity to respond remains, although it may be significantly impaired. There is a parallel in the psychological explanation of motivation (with which educated managers are likely to be more familiar) provided by Maslow's (1943) hierarchy of pre-potency of motives. Every management diploma student will recall that it is based upon a paradox: the most vital and necessary needs, for food and shelter, are not active motivators in complex, developed, and stable societies. Although these two accounts are launched from different perspectives, and although one of them is concerned with a different purpose, they both help to free us from the belief that because economic achievement efficiently attained is a necessary goal it follows that our behaviour is determined by it or that our actions are conditioned. We are, at least to some extent, free.

It is the despair of managers and their advisers that they have known that subordinate workers are free; unenclosed in their organizations to the extent that they can strike, leave, be late, withdraw their commitment, and occasionally engage in sabotage. Managers, we have learned more recently, also tend to serve their own ends, although their strategies of independence are conducted more covertly. Several behavioural scientists have proposed that this gap between the organization's needs and the individual's can be closed. Argyris has argued that the demands of hierarchical bureaucracy are inimical to the psychological health of employees and that their respective manoeuvres are necessary to their own survival. He and others have therefore advised the re-structuring of work and organization so as to give them a more human and satisfying form so that the circle may be squared. The intention is 'to increase the amount of psychological energy available for work' (Argyris 1964: 89), the purpose 'to understand the charges that the organisation (and the individual) will have to make if it is to obtain the most possible human energy for productive effort' (1964: 11–12). But such programmes of organizational reform can be seen as intended further to subsume the subordinate under the control of the employer, a control that will rest so lightly as to be unobserved and, therefore, irresistible. They are dangerous and transparent because human needs remain instrumental to economic ends. They claim to succeed in squaring the circle because they assume (or pretend to assume) that the ends of economic organization and the needs of human beings can be identified. No organization has ever succeeded in meeting the needs of its human inhabitants. Carlyle's idealized account of the Abbey of St Edmondsbury acknowledged that 'Abbot Samson found all men more or less headstrong, irrational, prone to disorder; continually threatening to prove *un*governable' (Carlyle 1960: 196). The modern hospital, committed as it is to the overarching devotion to patient care, is fissured by a network of professional, group, and personal interests. Any academic employed in a university, particularly at the present time, will acknowledge that the search for truth may be obscured by more immediate and individual or departmental concerns. The same is at least likely to be true of Ford Motors, from the top of its directing board to the semi-skilled black worker on the track. To pretend that these disparities of need can be met by organizational change that is directed at the achievement of economic ends is an evasion, deceptive to the extent that it is cynical.

In suggesting that managers should be taught to take into account responsibility for communities of human inhabitants, are we not in danger of falling into the same trap? That would be the case if I were to suggest that their concern with their function of community government will lead to improved performance, if it were to be made instrumental to the achievement of greater efficiency. But that is not the intention. The proposition is merely (it is sufficiently grandiose as it is) that the foundation of managerial authority, its legitimation by those subordinate to it, cannot be assured by any other means than the acceptance by management of its responsibility to the general community and for the government of its own. Efficiency and profit must be secured by other means, some of them likely to promote the anger and resistance of sections of the community that management must govern. Abbot Samson faced the same problem, but he *was* the acknowledged and authoritative leader of his community. The government of a country, as long as that country remains governable, will continue to exercise authority conceded to it by a community divided by a myriad of sectional interests while the measures taken by that government for the collection of taxes or the enforcement of law may be resisted.

The authority of management must rest upon a moral base, secure in a concern for the integrity and the good of the community that it governs. That authority must be achieved, won rather than imposed; it cannot be sought by coercion or by the deceptive application of psychological tricks. In this respect, behavioural science will be as ineffective as scientific management. Real authority must rest upon real moral concern, perceived to be real because its intentions are real. It may, it must be acknowledged, contribute to greater reciprocal commitment but that must not be its purpose. It is a paradox rather than a contradiction: John Ruskin repeatedly pointed out that you will achieve good work by not setting out to command it.

I have arrived at another paradox. I began with a criticism of Professor Wiener's argument that our ills were to be attributed to gentrification, to the damaging persistence of squirearchical values in an industrial society. I conclude with the suggestion that the moral reciprocity of pre-industrial society, the acknowledgement of rights and duties, and the concern to exercise care for a community by its leaders may be singularly relevant to our present condition. If only Professor Wiener were right, if only we remained under the influence of a persistent tradition and original forms of paternalism, if only we had succeeded in translating those values into the contemporary world, we might have made a better showing in it. Unfortunately, Professor Wiener was wrong.

References

Anthony, P. D. (1977) *The Ideology of Work.* London: Tavistock.

Argyris, C. (1964) *Integrating the Individual and the Organization.* New York: John Wiley.

Astley, W. G. (1984) Subjectivity, Sophistry and Symbolism in Management Science. *Journal of Management Studies* 21(3): 259–72.

Bailey, J. (1983) *Job Design and Work Organization.* London: Prentice Hall.

Batstone, E. (1984) *Working Order: Workplace Industrial Relations over Two Decades.* Oxford: Basil Blackwell.

Bendix, R. (1956) *Work and Authority in Industry.* New York: John Wiley.

Bensman, J. and Gerver, I. (1963) Crime and Punishment in the Factory. *American Sociological Review* 8(4).

Berg, M. (1980) *The Machinery Question and the Making of Political Economy, 1815–48.* Cambridge: Cambridge University Press.

Berle, A. and Means, G. (1932) *The Modern Corporation and Private Property.* New York: Macmillan.

Beynon, H. (1973) *Working for Ford.* Harmondsworth: Penguin.

Braverman, H. (1974) *Labour and Monopoly Capitalism.* New York: Monthly Review Press.

Brown, W. (1972) A Consideration of Custom and Practice: *British Journal of Industrial Relations* 10(1): 42–61.

Bruce, E. (1983) *Quaker Paternalism as a Model of Employer Relations.* University College, Cardiff. Unpublished undergraduate dissertation.

Bullock Committee (1977) *Industrial Democracy: Committee of Inquiry Report.* London: HMSO Cmnd 6706.

Burnham, J. (1941) *The Managerial Revolution.* London: Pitman.

Burns, T. (1977) *The B.B.C.* London: Macmillan.

—— (1981) *A Comparative Study of Administrative Structure and Organisational Processes in Selected Areas of the National Health Service.* Social Science Research Council Report, HRP 6725.

Carlyle, T. (1960) *Past and Present.* London: Dent.

CBI (Confederation of British Industry) (1980) *Trades Unions in a Changing World: the Challenge of Management.* London.

Chapman, S. D. (1967) *The Early Factory Masters.* London: David & Charles.

Child, J. (1969) *British Management Thought.* London: Allen & Unwin.

Child, J. and Patridge, B. (1982) *Lost Managers: Supervision in Industry and Society.* Cambridge: Cambridge University Press.

Child, J., Fores, M., Glover, I., and Lawrence, P. (1983) Professionalisation and Work Organisation in Britain and West Germany. *Sociology* 17(1): 63–78.

Clegg, H. A. (1970) *The System of Industrial Relations in Great Britain.* Oxford: Basil Blackwell.

Crichton, A. (1968) *Personnel Management in Context.* London: Batsford.

Dahrendorf, R. (1959) *Class and Class Conflict in Industrial Society.* London: Routledge & Kegan Paul.

Dalton, M. (1959) *Men who Manage.* New York: John Wiley.

Donovan (1968) *Report of the Royal Commission on Trade Unions and Employers' Associations.* London: HMSO Cmnd 3623.

Drucker, P. F. (1965) *The Future of Industrial Man.* New York: Mentor.

—— (1968) *The Practice of Management.* London: Pan.

Dunkerley, D. and Salaman, G. (eds) (1982) *The International Yearbook of Organization Studies, 1981.* London: Routledge & Kegan Paul.

Earl, M. J. (1983) Accounting in Management. In M. J. Earl (ed.) *Perspectives in Management.* Oxford: Oxford University Press.

Edwardes, M. (1984) *Back from the Brink.* London: Pan.

Edwards, R. (1978) *Contested Terrain.* London: Heinemann.

Fogarty, M. P. (1963) An Independent Comment. *Personnel Management.* XLX (363): 87.

Foster, J. (1977) *Class Struggle and the Industrial Revolution: Early Industrial Capitalism in three English Towns.* London: Methuen.

Fox, A. (1974a) *Beyond Contract: Work, Power and Trust Relations.* London: Faber & Faber.

—— (1974b) *Man Mismanagement.* London: Hutchinson.

—— (1985) *History and Heritage: The Social Origins of the British Industrial Relations System.* London: Allen & Unwin.

Gallie, D. (1978) *In Search of the New Working Class.* Cambridge: Cambridge University Press.

Garside, W. R. and Gospel, H. (1982) Employers and Managers: Their Organizational Structure and Changing Industrial Strategies. In C. Wrigley (ed.) *A History of British Industrial Relations, 1875–1914.* Brighton: Harvester Press.

Genovese, F. D. (1975) *Roll Jordan Roll.* London: Andre Deutsch.

Giddens, A. (1979) *Central Problems in Social Theory.* London: Macmillan.

—— (1981) *A Contemporary Critique of Historical Materialism.* London: Macmillan.

Glasgow Media Group (1976). *Bad News.* London: Routledge & Kegan Paul.

Goodman, J. F. B., Armstrong, E. J. A., Davis, J. E., and Wagner, A. (1977) *Rule Making and Industrial Peace.* London: Croom Helm.

Goodrich, C. (1920) *The Frontier of Control.* London: G. Bell. Published 1975 London: Pluto Press.

Gospel, H. (1983) The Development of Management Organization in Industrial Relations: An Historical Perspective. In K. Thurley and S. Woods (eds) *Industrial Relations and Management Strategy,* Cambridge: Cambridge University Press.

Gouldner, A. W. (1955) *Wildcat Strike.* London: Routledge & Kegan Paul.

—— (1960) The Norm of Reciprocity. *American Sociological Review* 25(2): 161–79.

Gowler, D. and Legge, K. (1983) The Meaning of Management and the Management of Meaning. In M. J. Earl (ed.) *Perspectives in Management.* Oxford: Oxford University Press.

Hardy, B. (1975) *Tellers and Listeners: The Narrative Imagination.* London: Athlone Press.

Herman, S. M. (1968) *The People Specialists.* New York: Knopf.

Hyman, R. (1972) *Strikes.* London: Fontana.

IPM (Institute of Personnel Management) (1985) *National Conference Programme* October.

IS (Industrial Society) (1978) *Why Industry Matters.* London: Industrial Society.

—— (1980) *Explaining the Economic Facts.* London: Industrial Society.

Jackson, P. W. (1985) An Analysis of the Nature and Influence of

Paternalist Management in the Nineteenth Century. University of Wales. Incomplete thesis.

Keenoy, T. (1985) *Invitation to Industrial Relations*. Oxford: Basil Blackwell.

Kotter, J. P. (1982) *The General Manager*. New York: Collier-Macmillan.

Lane, T. and Roberts, K. (1971) *Strike at Pilkingtons*. London: Collins/Fontana.

Leavitt, H. J. (1983) *Management and Management Education in the West: What's Right and What's Wrong*. London: London Business School. The Stockton Lecture.

Legge, K. (1978) *Power, Innovation and Problem-solving in Personnel Management*. Maidenhead: McGraw-Hill.

Littler, C. (1983) *The Development of the Labour Process in Capitalist Societies*. London: Routledge & Kegan Paul.

MacIntyre, A. (1981) *After Virtue: a Study in Moral Theory*. London: Duckworth.

Maslow, A. H. (1943) A Theory of Human Motivation. *Psychological Review* 40: 370–96.

McKenna, F. (1980) *The Railway Workers, 1840–1970*. London: Faber & Faber.

Melling, J. (1982) Men in the Middle or Men on the Margin? In D. Dunkerley and G. Salaman (eds) *The International Yearbook of Organization Studies, 1981*. London: Routledge & Kegan Paul.

Mills, C. W. (1956) *White Collar: The American Middle Classes*. Oxford: Oxford University Press.

Moore, R. (1974) *Pit-men, Preachers and Politics*. Cambridge: Cambridge University Press.

Nichols, T. and Beynon, H. (1977) *Living with Capitalism: Class Relations and the Modern Factory*. London: Routledge & Kegan Paul.

Niven, M. M. (1967) *Personnel Management, 1913–1963*. London: Institute of Personnel Management.

Nock, O. S. (1955) *The Railway Engineers*. London: Batsford.

Pahl, R. E. (1984) *Divisions of Labour*. Oxford: Basil Blackwell.

Parker, P. (1983) How I See the Personnel Function. *Personnel Management* 15(1): 16–19.

Peel, M. (1984) *Management Development and Training: A Survey of Current Policy and Practice*. London: Professional Publications.

Peters, T. J. and Waterman, R. H. (1982) *In Search of Excellence: Lessons from America's Best-Run Companies*. New York: Harper & Row.

Petrie, D. J. (1965) The Personnel 'Professionals'. Who Needs Them? *Personnel Management* XLVII, 373: 162–64.

Pettigrew, A. (1985) *The Awakening Giant: Continuity and Change in I.C.I.* Oxford: Basil Blackwell.

Pollard, S. (1965) *The Genesis of Modern Management*. London: Edward Arnold.

Redfield, R. (1960) *The Little Community* and *Peasant Society and Culture*. Toronto: University of Chicago Press.

Reed, M. (1985) *Redirections in Organizational Analysis*. London: Tavistock.

Report of the Royal Commission on Trade Unions and Employers' Associations (1968). London: HMSO Cmnd 3623.

Roberts, D. (1979) *Paternalism in Early Victorian England*. London: Croom Helm.

Rose, H. (1970) *Management Education in the 1970s: Growth and Issues*. London: HMSO.

Rothblatt, S. (1981) *The Revolution of the Dons: Cambridge and Society in Victorian England*. Cambridge: Cambridge University Press.

Ruskin, J. (1905) *Unto This Last*. In E. T. Cooke and A. Wedderburn (eds) *The Works of John Ruskin*, Library Edition, vol. 17. London: George Allen.

Salaman, G. (1982) Managing the Frontier of Control. In A. Giddens and G. MacKenzie (eds) *Social Class and the Division of Labour*. Cambridge: Cambridge University Press.

Simon, H. A. (1976) *Administrative Behaviour*. New York: Collier Macmillan.

Smiles, S. (ed.) (1891) *James Nasmyth, Engineer: an Autobiography*. London: John Murray.

Stewart, R. (1982) *Choices for the Manager: A guide to managerial work and behaviour*. Maidenhead: McGraw-Hill.

—— (1983) Managerial Behaviour: How Research has Changed the Traditional Picture. In M. J. Earl (ed.) *Perspectives in Management*. Oxford: Oxford University Press.

Storey, J. (1981) *The Challenge to Management Control*. London: Business Books.

—— (1983) *Managerial Prerogatives and the Question of Control*. London: Routledge & Kegan Paul.

Taylor, F. W. (1911) *Scientific Management*. New York: Harper.

Thompson, E. P. (1968) *The Making of the English Working Class*. Harmondsworth: Penguin.

Thompson, P. (1983) *The Native of Work*. London: Macmillan.

TUC (1944) *Report on Post-War Reconstruction*. London: Trades Union Congress.

Unwin, G., Hulme, A., and Taylor, G. (1924) *Samuel Oldknow and the Arkwrights*. Manchester: Manchester University Press.

Urwick, L. and Brech, E. F. L. (1957) *The Making of Scientific Management*. vol. 2. London: Pitman.

Watson, T. J. (1983) *Towards a General Theory of Personnel Management and Industrial Relations Management.* Trent Business School. Occasional Paper.

Watt, E. D. (1982) *Authority.* London: Croom Helm.

Whitley, R., Thomas, A., and Marceau, J. (1981) *Masters of Business? Business Schools and Business Graduates in Britain and France.* London: Tavistock.

Wiener, M. J. (1981) *English Culture and the Decline of the Industrial Spirit, 1850–1980.* Cambridge: Cambridge University Press.

Williams, I. A. (1931) *The Firm of Cadbury, 1831–1931.* London: Constable.

Winkler, J. T. (1974) The Ghost at the Bargaining Table. *British Journal of Industrial Relations* 12(2): 191–212.

Name index

Subject index